I0786302

Current Superstitions

Collected from the Oral Tradition of English Speaking Folk

by Fanny D. Bergen

with an introduction by Dahlia V. Nightly

This work contains material that was originally published in 1896.

This publication is within the Public Domain.

*This edition is reprinted for entertainment purposes
and in accordance with all applicable Federal and International Laws.*

Introduction Copyright 2018 by Dahlia V. Nightly

CREDITS & ACKNOWLEDGEMENTS

Front Cover -
Skull in a Niche by Barthel Bruyn the Elder
[Public Domain],
via Wikimedia Commons

Back Cover -
Fotomorgana-Grad Kamen by Andraz Muljavec (*Fotomorgana*)
[CC BY-SA 4.0 - https://creativecommons.org/licenses/by-sa/4.0],
via Wikimedia Common

Black Books Logo -
Candle Collection by VectorPocket, via FreePik.com *(Cropped)*
Vanitas [Painting] by Bartholomäus Bruyn the Elder, Public Domain *(Cropped)*
Marbled Pedestal with Old Books by Kues1, via FreePik.com (Cropped)

Research / Sources -
Wikimedia Commons
www.Commons.Wikimedia.org

Many thanks to all the incredible photographers, artists,
researchers, and archivists who share their great work.

PLEASE NOTE :
As with all reprinted books of this age that are intended to perfectly reproduce the
original edition, considerable pains and effort had to be undertaken to correct fading and
sometimes outright damage to existing proofs of this title. At times, this task can be quite
monumental, requiring an almost total rebuilding of some pages from digital proofs of
multiple copies. Despite this, imperfections still sometimes exist in the final proof and
may detract slightly from the visual appearance of the text.

DISCLAIMER :
Due to the age of this book, some methods or practices may have been deemed unsafe or
unacceptable in the interim years. In utilizing the information herein, you do so at your
own risk. We republish antiquarian books without judgment or revisionism, solely for
their historical and cultural importance, and for educational purposes.

Introduction

We at *Black Books* are pleased to bring you this special edition of a fabulous old text on superstitions in the oral tradition.

This special edition of ***Current Superstitions Collected from the Oral Tradition of English Speaking Folk*** was written by Fanny D. Bergen, and first published in 1896, making it over 120 years old.

This antiquarian text explores the word-of-mouth folklore and superstitions handed down through the generations of English-speaking people.

The book runs the gamut of topics including *Babyhood, Childhood, Physical Characteristics, Halloween and Other Festivals, Love and Marriage, Money, Cures, Mortuary Customs*, and more.

This fantastic old find is an absolute must-have for all those interested in oral history traditions in general, and in age-old English language superstitions in particular.

Strangely yours...

~ *Dahlia V. Nightly*

State of Jefferson, July 2018

PREFACE.

In the "Popular Science Monthly" for July, 1886, there was printed a somewhat miscellaneous assortment of customs and superstitions under the title: *Animal and Plant Lore of Children.* This article was in the main composed of reminiscences of my own childhood spent in Northern Ohio, though two or three friends of New England rearing contributed personal recollections. Seldom is a line cast which brings ashore such an abundant catch as did my initial folk-lore paper. A footnote had, by the advice of a friend, been appended asking readers to send similar lore to the writer. About seventy answers were received, from all sorts of localities, ranging from Halifax to New Orleans. These numerous letters convinced me that there was even then, before the foundation of the national Society, a somewhat general interest in folk-lore, — not a scientific interest, but a fondness for the subject-matter itself. Many who do not care for folk-lore as a subject of research are pleased to have recalled to them the fancies, beliefs, and customs of childhood and early youth. (A single proverb, superstition, riddle, or tradition may, by association of ideas, act like a magic mirror in bringing back hundreds of long-forgotten people, pastimes, and occupations. And whatever makes one young, if only for an hour, will ever fascinate.) The greater number of those who kindly responded to the request for additional notes to my animal and plant lore were naturally those of somewhat literary or scientific tastes and pursuits. Many letters were from teachers, many others from physicians, a few from professional scientists, the rest from men and women of various callings, who had been pleased by suggestions that aroused memories of the credulous and unreflecting period in their own lives. The abundant material thus brought in, which consisted of folk-lore items of the most varied kind, was read gratefully and with pleasant surprise.

The items were assorted and catalogued after some provisional fashion of my own. Succeeding papers issued in the " Popular Science Monthly " brought in further accessions. I gradually formed the habit of asking, as opportunity offered, any one and every one for folk-lore. Nurses abound in such knowledge. Domestic help, whether housekeepers, seamstresses, or servants, whether American or foreign, all by patient questioning were induced to give of their full store.

The folk-lorist who chances to have a pet superstition or two of his own that he never fails to observe, has an open-sesame to beliefs of this sort held by any one with whom he comes in contact. The fact that I have (I blush to confess it) a preference for putting on my right shoe before the left has, I dare say, been the providential means of bringing to me hundreds of bits of folk-lore. Many times has the exposure of this weakness instantly opened up an opportunity for asking questions about kindred customs and superstitions. I once asked an Irish peasant girl from County Roscommon if she could tell me any stories about fairies. "Do ye give in to fairies then, ma'am?" she joyously asked, adding, "A good many folks don't give in to them " (believe in them, *i. e.*, the fairies). Apparently she was heartily glad to meet some one who spoke her own language. From that hour she was ever ready to tell me tales or recall old sayings and beliefs about the doings and powers of the "good people" of old Ireland.

A stewardess, properly approached, can communicate a deal of lore in her leisure hours during a three or four days' ocean trip. Oftentimes a caller has by chance let drop a morsel that was quickly picked up and preserved.

The large amount of botanical and zoölogical mythology that has gradually accumulated in my hands is reserved for separate treatment. Now and then some individual item of the sort appears in the following pages, but only for some special reason. A considerable proportion of my general folk-lore was orally collected from persons of foreign birth. There were among these more Irish than of any other one nationality, but Scotch and English were somewhat fully represented, and Scandinavians (including one Icelander), Italians, a Syrian, a Parsee, and several Japanese contributed to the collection.

It has been a puzzling question to decide just where to draw the line in separating foreign from what we may call current American folk-lore. The traditions and superstitions that a mother as a child or girl heard in a foreign land, she tells her children born here, and the lore becomes, as it were, naturalized, though sometimes but little modified from the form in which it was current where the mother originally heard it. Whether to include any folk-lore collected from oral narrators or from correspondents, even if it had been very recently brought hither, was the question. At length it has been decided to print only items taken down from the narration of persons born in America, though frequent parallels and numberless variants have been obtained from persons now resident here, though reared in other countries.

It would be a most interesting task to collate the material embraced in the present collection with the few published lists of American superstitions, customs, and beliefs, and with the many dialect and other stories, the books of travel, local histories, and similar sources of information in regard to our own folk-lore. Equally valuable would be the endeavor to trace the genesis of the most important of the superstitions here set down. But the limits of the present publication make any such attempt wholly out of the question, and the brief notes which are appended refer to but a few of the matters which invite comment and discussion.

Some few repetitions have been almost unavoidable, since not infrequently a superstition might consistently be classified under more than one head; besides, it is not unusual to find that varied significations are attributed to the same act, accident, or coincidence. When localities are wanting it is sometimes because the narrator could not tell where he had become familiar with the items communicated; again, a chance correspondent failed to note the locality. In putting on paper these popular beliefs and notions, the abbreviated, often rather elliptical, vernacular in which they are passed about from mouth to mouth has to a great extent been followed.

It is impossible here to name the legion of individuals from whom the subject-matter of the various chapters of this volume has been gathered. But thanks are especially due to the following persons, who have contributed largely to the contents of the book: —

Charles Aldrich, Webster City, Iowa.

Miss Ellen Beauchamp, Baldwinsville, N. Y.

John G. Bourke, Capt. 3d Cavalry U. S. A., Ft. Ethan Allen, Vt.

Miss M. A. Caller, A. C. F. College, Tuskeegee, Ala.

Preface.

John S. Caulkins, M. D., Thornville, Mich.
Miss Ellen Chase, Brookline, Mass.
Miss Ruth R. Cronyn, Bernardston, Mass.
Uriah A. Greene, Flint, Mich.
Professor George M. Harmon, Tufts College, Mass.
W. J. McGee, U. S. Geol. Survey, Washington, D. C.
Hector McInnes, Halifax, N. S.
John B. Nichols, Washington, D. C.
John G. Owens,[1] Lewisburg, Pa.
Prof. Frederick Reed, Talladega, Ala.
Mrs. Amanda M. Thrush, Plymouth, O.
Miss Helen S. Thurston, Providence, R. I.
Rev. A. C. Waghorne, New Harbor, N. F.
Miss Susan Hayes Ward, "The Independent," New York, N. Y.
Miss Ellen L. Wickes, Chestertown, Md.

Above all am I indebted to Mr. Newell, whose generous coöperation and advice have been invaluable to one working under peculiar hindrances.

FANNY D. BERGEN.

CAMBRIDGE, MASS., 1. 15. 1896.

[1] Deceased.

CONTENTS.

Contents.

CURRENT SUPERSTITIONS.

INTRODUCTION.

THE record contained in the present volume forms the first considerable printed collection made in America of superstitions belonging to English-speaking folk. Numerous as are the items here presented, only a part of the matter is included, the collector having preferred to reserve for separate presentation superstitions connected with animal and plant lore, material which would require a space about equal to that here occupied. Again, the present gathering by no means pretends to completeness; while certain departments may be adequately represented, other sections exhibit scarce more than a gleaning. The collection, therefore, will be looked on as a first essay, subject to revision and enlargement.

The designations of locality will suffice to show the width of the area from which information has been obtained, as well as the degree of similarity which appears in the folk-lore of different regions belonging to this wide territory. Here and there may be observed items showing a measure of originality; a new superstition may have arisen, or an ancient one been modified, according to the fancy of an individual, in consequence of defective memory, or in virtue of misapprehension. But on the whole such peculiarities make no figure, nor does recent immigration play any important part. Almost the entire body of this tradition belongs to the English stock; it is the English population which, together with the language, has imposed on other elements of American life its polity, society, ethics, and tradition.

This relation is not an isolated phenomenon; on the contrary, it is entirely in the line of experience. Language is the most important factor which determines usage and influences character; this result is effected through the literature, oral or written, with which, in virtue of the possession of a particular speech, any given people is brought into contact. In this process race goes for little. Borrowing the tongue of a superior race, a subject population receives also the songs, tales, habits, inclinations which go with the speech ; human nature, in all times essentially imitative, copies qualities which are united with presumed superiority ; to this process not even racial hostility is a bar ; assimilation and transmission go on in spite of hatred directed against the persons who are the object of the imitation ; such a process may be observed in the recent history of Ireland.

Reception of new ideas, however, though promoted by the possession of a common language constituting a means of exchange, is not limited by its absence ; on the contrary, in all historical time among contiguous races takes place a transference of ideas which dislike and even warfare do not prevent. Here the law seems to be that the lower culture has relatively little effect on the higher with which it is in contact, while the superior civilization speedily influences an inferior one. Nor is the effect confined to the higher classes of any given society ; beginning with these, the new knowledge descends through all ranks, and everywhere carries its transforming influence. What is true of written literature in a less degree is true of oral ; songs and tales, rites and customs, beliefs and superstitions, diffuse themselves from the civilization which happens to be in fashion, with a rapidity greater or less according to the interworking of a multitude of modifying forces. In the other direction, from the lower culture to the higher, exchange is slow, albeit likely to be promoted, in certain cases, by peculiar conditions, such as the deliberate literary choice which seeks opportunity for archaistic representation, or the respect which an advanced race may have for the magical ability of a simple tribe, believed to be nearer to nature, and therefore more likely to remain in communion with natural forces.

But these exceptional effects are of small relative moment ; the general principle, continually at work, in the main controls the result. In regard to the themes of stories especially, the many tongues and dialects of Western Europe offer scarcely more variation than will be often found to exist among the versions of the same tale which may be discovered in a single canton. The spirit of the language, already mentioned as constituting the element of nationality, taking possession of this common stock of knowledge, moulds its precise form and sentiment in accordance with its own character ; it is in details, rather than in outlines, that racial differences are found to exist ; this principle applies in a considerable degree in the field of folk-tales, even between cultures so opposite as those of Western Europe and Western Africa.

In the case of superstitions, the diffusive process, though less rapid or effectual than in tales, is nevertheless continually active ;

in Europe, at least, a similar identity will probably be discovered. But in this category the problem of separating what is general, because human, from that which is common, because diffused, always a complicated task, will be found more difficult than in literary matter, and without the aid of extensive collection insoluble. It is possible to fall back on the consideration that, after all, such resolution matters not very much, since in any case the survival of the belief indicates its humanity, and for the purpose of the study of human nature borrowed superstitions may be cited as confidently as if original in the soil to which they have emigrated, and where they have indissolubly intertwined themselves with thought and habit.

Again, it is to be considered that while differences of speech impede, but do not prevent integration, changes of condition may have an immediate effect in producing differentiation. Protestantism, by banishing complicated usages connected with sacred days, has caused English folk-lore to vary from Continental ; so far this contrast seems a result of the alterations of the last three hundred years, rather than of more remote inconsistency.

If these remarks are in any degree valid, it follows that from the presence or absence of any particular item of belief in this or that English-speaking district no conclusion is to be drawn ; the deficiency must be supposed to proceed from absence of record, and seldom to depend on the structure of the population. To this general doctrine, as usual with such propositions, may be observed minor exceptions. Whatever doubts may be cast on the operation of the principle as applicable to England, there can be no doubt that it is valid in the United States and Canada.

It is not, however, intended to assert that the contributions of the entire region covered in this collection are identical in character. On the contrary, it will be seen that the record made in certain districts, as for example in Newfoundland and among the Mountain Whites of the Alleghanies, presents superstition as more primitive and active than in the eastern United States. But this vitality is only to be regarded as the persistence of a stock once proper to English-speaking folk, and by no means as indicating a diversity of origins.

The chief value of a collection such as the present consists in the light it may be made to cast on the history of mental processes ; in other words, on its psychologic import.

To appreciate this value, it is needful to understand the quality in which superstition really consists. This distinguishing characteristic is obscured by the definitions of English dictionaries, which describe superstition as a disease, depending on an excess of religious sentiment, which disposes the person so affected to unreasonable credulity.   In the same spirit, it has been the wont of divines to characterize superstition and unbelief as opposite poles, between which lies the golden mean of discreet faith.   But this view is inadequate and erroneous.

The manner of conception mentioned has been borrowed from Latin and Greek writers of the Roman republic and of the Imperial period.   In primitive Roman usage, *superstitio* and *religio* were synonyms; both, perhaps, etymologically considered, expressed no more than that habit of careful consideration with which a prudent man will measure the events which encounter him, and determine his conduct with a view to consequences.   *Superstitio* may have indicated only the *overstanding* of the phenomenon, the pause necessary for its deliberate inspection.   By Cicero a distinction was made; the word was now employed to designate a state of mind under the influence of supernatural terrors.   In the Greek tongue a similar conception was expressed by the word *deisidaimonia,* or fear of dæmons, a term in bad odor as associated with practices of Oriental temple worship representing primitive conceptions, and therefore odious to later and more enlightened Hellenic thought.   Established as a synonym of the Greek noun, *superstitio* received all the meaning which Plutarch elaborated as to the former; the idea of that excellent heathen, that true piety is the mean between atheism and credulity, has given a sense to the word superstition, and become a commonplace of Christian hortatory literature.

It is, however, sufficiently obvious that the signification mentioned does not have application to the omens recorded in the present volume, the majority of which have no direct connection with spiritual beings, while it will also be allowed that these do not lie without the field ordinarily covered by the word superstition.   For our purposes, therefore, it is necessary to enlarge this definition. This may be done by emphasizing the first component part of the word, and introducing into it the notion of what has been left over, or of survival, made familiar by the genius of Edward B. Tylor.   In these lingering notions we have opinions respecting relations of cause and effect which have resulted as a necessary consequence from past intellectual conditions.   A superstition, accordingly, I should define as a belief respecting causal sequence, depending on reasoning proper to an outgrown culture.   According to this view, with adequate information it would be possible to trace the mental process in virtue of which arise such expectations of futurity, and to discover the methods of their gradual modification and eventual supersession by generalizations founded on experience more accurate and extensive.   Yet it is not to be assumed that in each and every case such elucidation will be possible.   In all human conduct there is an element which cannot be designated otherwise than as accidental; this uncertainty appears to be greater, the reaction against the natural conditions less definite, the more primitive is the life. It is impossible to forecast in what manner a savage may be impressed by an event of which he can note only external conditions, or how his action may respond to the impression. One may guess what opinion an augur would form concerning the appearance of a single eagle or raven; but it would be labor lost to attempt to conjecture the manner in which the imagination of the observer would explain a flight of these birds, or what complicated rules augural art might evolve to guide the interpretation.

This accidental quality, and the arbitrariness with which phenomena are judged to be ominous, will be visible in the numerous "signs" here recorded. At first sight, it may be thought that extreme folly is their salient quality. Yet if we take a wide view the case is reversed; we are surprised, not at the unintelligibility of popular belief, but at its simplicity, and at the frequency with which we can discern the natural process of unsystematic conjecture. Such judgments are not to be treated with derision, as subjects of ridicule, but to be seriously examined, as revealing the natural procedure of intelligence limited to a superficial view of phenomena.

This consideration leads to an important remark. (The term survival expresses a truth, but only a part of the truth. Usages, habits, opinions, which are classed as superstition, exhibit something more than the unintelligent and unconscious persistence of habit. Folklore survives, and popular practices continue, only so long as endures a method of thinking corresponding to that in which these had their origin. Individual customs may be preserved simply as a matter of thoughtless habit; yet in general it is essential that these usages should be related to conscious intellectual life; so soon as they cease to be so explicable, they begin to pass into oblivion.)

The chapters of this collection, therefore, will emphasize the doctrine that the essential elements of human nature continue to exist, however opposite may be the actions in which its operations are manifested. In examining many of the maxims of conduct here set forth, we are able to understand the motives in which they had their being; we perceive that the inclination has not disappeared, however checked by mediation through complex experience, and however counteracted by the weight of later maxims. The examiner finds that he himself shares the mental state of the superstitious person; if not, he can easily make an effort of imagination which will enable him to comprehend its evident reasonableness. Thus, while superstitions are properly designated as survivals, it will in many cases be found that they represent a survival of ratiocination as well as of action.

In some striking examples, also, it happens that the modern notion indicates the continuance of conceptions more ancient than a mass of connected ideas which have wholly perished. The former endure, because, being simple in their nature, they represent a human impulse, an impulse which animated the prehistoric ancestor as well as the modern descendant. When this tendency ceases to operate, the plant suddenly withers. (So it is that an elimination of these beliefs, which formed the science of remote antiquity, has taken place in our own century, which has worked a change greater than fifty preceding generations, because it has been able to introduce generalizations with which ancient notions and habits are perceived no longer to coincide.)

As illustrations of the psychologic value of the material, it may be permitted to offer brief comments on the several sections.

In the usages of mothers and nurses, it is interesting to observe with what persistence survives the conception that the initial action of the series determines the character of events sequent in order. It is still a universal practice to consecrate every baby by a rite not ecclesiastical. The infant, on his first journey, must be taken to a height symbolic of his future fortune, an elevation believed to secure the prosperity of his whole subsequent career. It would be of interest to learn what analogies the practice has among races in a primitive condition of culture. The babe of the Pueblo of Sia, when on the fourth day (four being a sacred number) for the first time he is taken from the dark chamber, is ritually presented to his father the Sun; similarly, in a superstition of the present series (I know not how generally observed) Sunday is said to be the day on which the infant is first to be carried into the sunshine. It is likely that such continuing customs represent feeble echoes of pre-Christian dedicatory ceremonies, which in the first instance were themselves founded on a corresponding habit of thought ; according to an opposite, yet connected system of notions, we find Protestant Christianity still preserving a memento of the world-old and universal belief in a crowd of malicious spirits, prepared at every moment to take up their residence in the convenient shelter of the human frame, as a hermit crab watches for a suitable shell in which to make his home. It must be owned that the volume of observances connected with infancy, here presented, is very inadequate ; it is certain that a nurse of a century ago would have been familiar with a vastly more extensive array of duties and cautions. As we go back in time and culture, action becomes more restricted. Where the effects of any line of conduct are unknown, adherence to precedent is all-important ; every part of the life must be administered according to a complicated system of rules, while common prudence is considered as inseparable from religious obligation.

The following section presents us with interesting material, in the exhibition of ideas and customs which are maintained by children themselves, and which they learn from one another rather than from their elders. It is true that these are of necessity the reflection of the conceptions and practice of older persons ; but, according to the law of their nature, it is found that children often exhibit a peculiar conservatism, in virtue of which habits of thought still exercise control, which among men and women have been outgrown. This is illustrated in popular games and songs which children have orally preserved ; and the same is true of their superstitions. Women, especially, who may peruse this collection will be surprised to find how many of the items here recorded will seem familiar, and at the same time to have received credence ; in the case of a particularly clear-minded person, free from any disposition toward credulity, nearly a hundred of these superstitions were remembered. The ideas in question, perhaps at no time more than half believed, have frequently altogether faded into oblivion.

Attention should be paid, also, to the imaginative power of the youthful mind, and the manner in which beliefs are visualized, and appear as realities of perception. To illustrate this principle have been included a few examples belonging rather to individual than to general opinion. The little girl who without any direct instruction imagines that the light of the heaven gleams through the orifices we call stars, who sees celestial beings in meteor form winging their way across the skies, or who is surrounded by the benevolent spirits which her discriminating education, banishing the terrors of the supernatural world, has permitted to exist for her comprehension, illustrates that readiness of fancy and control of vision by expectation which belongs to humanity in the reverse degree of the reflective habit. Herein childish conceptions and vivacity of feeling represent the human faculty which education may control but cannot obliterate.

Beliefs relating to the influence of physiognomy present us with a very limited anthology of popular ideas, which in elaborate developments have been expanded into pseudo-sciences, and fill whole libraries of learned misinformation. These notions may be divided into two classes. On the one hand appear indications founded on natural analogies, as when we still speak of close-fistedness. On the other side, many of these associations are arbitrary, as when the study of spots on the nails is supposed to give means for determining future fortune. Such conclusions depend partly on the correct opinion that in the cradle lies the future man, with all elements of his complex nature, and partly on external marks, the interpretation of which is purely arbitrary.

The chapter on " Projects " presents the reader with a class of usages, sufficiently foolish when considered in themselves, but none the less demanding attention, as exhibiting, in full energy, the survival, at the end of the nineteenth century, of the practice of divination. It is true that these attempts to forecast the future are commonly made in a sportive manner and only with partial belief, being now for the most part reduced to social sports. They belong also almost exclusively to the female sex, who by way of amusement still keep up rites which are to determine the future partner in life. Yet that these observances were formerly performed with sober forethought may be seen by the superstitious character with which in retired districts they are still invested; it is likely that in this limited field we have the final echoes of ceremonies employed to determine action and to supply means for the estimation of every species of good or evil fortune. Among these customs a considerable part may be of relatively recent origin, but a number are undoubtedly ancient.

Particularly remarkable is the word by which in the English folk-lore of America, at least, these practices seem to have been popularly entitled. Dictionaries give no aid in explaining the signification of the word " project," here used in the sense of a ceremony of divination. I cannot offer any explanation as to the probable antiquity of the term ; neither middle-Latin nor Romance languages seem to offer parallels. One might guess that if all were known, the use might be found to proceed from the special language of mediæval magic or astrology (perhaps mirror-divination).

With practices of this sort has been connected an incident of colonial history. During the accusations brought against alleged witches of Salem, Massachusetts, in 1692, the chief agents were a group of " children " belonging to a particular neighborhood of that town. It has been asserted that these young persons, previous to the outbreak of the excitement, formed a " circle " of girls in the habit of meeting for the purpose of performing " magical tricks " (to use a phrase employed by Cotton Mather), and that it was experience so acquired that fitted them for the part afterwards played in the trials. This statement has been repeated by so many recent writers as to become a commonplace of accepted history ; it would seem, however, that the representation depends on the invention of a modern essayist, who transferred to the colonial period ideas derived from his acquaintance with the phenomena of contemporary spiritualistic *séances*, and that the habit of " trying projects," no doubt universal in colonial times, had nothing to do with the delusion in question. (See note, p. 153.)

Ancient popular divination would, as a matter of course, have taken a ritual character, and been associated especially with particular seasons. It is therefore more than an accident, that many of these harmless observations seem especially connected with Halloween. The Day of All Saints, of which name our English title is a translation, precedes that of All Souls; for the institution and significance of both the church has its explanation. Yet this account is not the correct one : these feasts descend, not from any Christian ecclesiastical ordination, but from an ancient festival of the dead; they represent the survival of a celebration which probably consisted in the bestowing on the departed, after the ingathering of the harvest, his share of the fruits of the ground, conveyed by direct material administration. That at such a period spirits of the dead should be supposed to walk the earth, would be a matter of course; in early time these would be conceived as returning in order to behold and join the sacred dances of the tribe. Accordingly, there seem to be indications showing an original association of some of these usages with the lower world; such may be the significance of the backward movement, or the inversion of garments, occasionally recommended. In order to put one's self in connection with the world of darkness, it is essential to reverse the procedure which is proper for the realm of light. This principle, appearing in mediæval magic, could also be illustrated from savage custom. It can hardly be doubted that the limitation of such forecasts to the field of choosing partners for life is but a survival of an older practice, in which divinations of fortune in other directions also were sought; on the day sacred to the dead, it may be that the latter, as having power and knowledge, were invoked to act as illuminators. The stress laid on dreams appears to imply a practice of evoking spirits, whether of the deceased or of the living.

In the division entitled "Love and Marriage" we are dealing not with ceremonies, but "signs;" in the former case a voluntary action is implied in the consulter of fate; in the latter, the subject is passive. The word "signs" is a popular term for omens of any kind; in this case we cannot be in error in seeking a Latin derivation, *signum* being classically used in this sense. Here, again, the prognostics in question are respected only by women, and at the present time, with but a light admixture of genuine credulity, unless among people of secluded districts, retaining old-world notions. Foolish as are these ideas of sequence, they indicate a habit of association anciently prevalent, which in early times had the most serious consequences.

The gathering of expectations relating to "Wishes" shows that the name and idea of folk-lore must not be limited to primitive beliefs, or to the ideas of uneducated persons. The assumption that an occurrence, neither unusual nor characterized by any correspondent quality, may promote the fulfilment of a contemporaneous desire, illustrates the arbitrary nature of a considerable part of this lore. Nevertheless, it cannot be doubted that many of these beliefs, if they could be followed back to their origins, would be found to exhibit some process of consistent though erroneous reasoning, as exhibited in the case of wishes made with reference to the state of the moon, hereafter to be mentioned. It is also to be observed that prayer to the evening star forms a feature of the usages in question.

Of dreams we are presented with a series in some degree representing their function in surviving belief. The comparison of these with dream books, still sold and used, and with a more extensive collection of superstitions, retained in this and other continents, would no doubt offer curious results. At present attention may be called only to one remarkable trait, namely : the interpretation of dreams by contraries. This practice I conceive to be altogether modern, and to have resulted from the extension of scientific culture, which has lead to the discredit of more direct explanations. So far as I am aware, dreams in literature, ancient or mediæval, are always presumed symbolically to represent the future, and to be capable of straightforward interpretation.

The usages of folk-medicine form a wide subject, which would occupy many volumes such as the present ; a mere bibliography of the literature could not be included in the number of pages here allowed. The gleaning, also, is in this case very imperfect ; the greater number of such " Cures " would fall in that part of the subject here omitted, relating to the function of animals and plants. In this field, conceptions formerly operative have not yet disappeared ; " the doctrine of signatures," that is to say, the rule that the healing object is indicated by its resemblance to the organ affected, has scarcely passed into oblivion, while popular systems of treatment are still based on rules not essentially different. In addition to this guiding idea, an exorcistic method has survived ; in our folk-lore is retained the removal of the trouble in virtue of its transfer to another place or person. Especially in the significant case of warts, such rule of early medicine operates with full force. Here, as in other instances, the obscure influence of suggestion plays a complicated part ; belief in the efficacy of any system of treatment appears sufficient to promote its effect. These charms are perhaps sometimes effective, even although no conscious attention is paid to the process ; but to enter on this field would be foreign to the present discussion. It is sufficient to point out that in popular belief the preservation of the theory goes hand in hand with the survival of the practice.

Weather proverbs form an extensive body of popular observations, here only partially recorded. From the psychologic point of view, the principal interest attaches to the mental causes of these prognostics. Collectors have generally assumed that in this field experience is at the basis of a great part of the alleged knowledge. It may be so with a few of the simpler signs; yet, even in respect to these, great diversity is visible. In general, I should myself attach small importance to this consideration. Remarkable in man regarded as an intellectual being is the variation to be observed in the effect of experience. In certain relations of daily life the savage is as quick to learn, and as accurate in his judgment, as civilized man; mention need only be made of his skill in the hunt, and his intimacy with the forest. But under complicated conditions, whenever this action falls outside of daily habit, he appears incapable of profiting by observation; on the contrary, it is usually <u>imagination</u> which dictates presumed experience. (The latter rarely corrects a superstition; as already remarked, discovery of error in the application of inherited theory is applied only to increase the complexity of the formula. Not until the existence of a means of record, and the formation of a body of observations capable of methodical arrangement, is an erroneous belief superseded, when the true causes of the events become manifest; of this principle ideas respecting the weather constitute good illustrations.

Students of this collection will be surprised by the number and vitality of formulas and beliefs relative to the moon. It is probable that the majority of the readers of the male sex will have no other associations with the newly born moon than that poetic sentiment which delights in the vision of the faint sickle silver through the twilight; if they possess any further association with the planet, it is likely to be no more than a vague dread of the effect of its radiance falling on a sleeper. Women, on the contrary, will remember that the moon should be first seen not "full face," but "over the the right shoulder;" they will be aware that with such vision may be united a wish, to which jesting fancy assigns a probability of accomplishment. But these, also, will be surprised by the discovery that lunar divination is maintained with profound seriousness, and that the honor paid to the orb is nothing else than a continued worship, still connected with material blessings expected from its bounty.

This record reveals the central principle and natural cause of moon worship, by making clear the effect still ascribed to the variation of the luminary. It is the night which is especially the season of primitive worship; from times long antecedent to written history, as well among the lowest savages as among tribes possessing the beginnings of civilization, changes of the starry heavens have been the object of devout contemplation and of reverent study. To the watcher it is the rapid growth of the lunar crescent that is the most distinctive feature of differences between the nights, an alteration which could not but be supposed to exercise control over human and animal life. According to natural processes of thought, it was inevitable that during the time when it so rapidly increases, and becomes dominant in the sky, the principle of growth should appear to prevail; and on the other hand, that the time of lunar diminution should be the season of decay. Hence the conclusion, probably prevalent in all times and countries, that designs and undertakings which expect increase should belong to the new moon, and that only operations which aim at the annihilation of existence should be carried on during the waning quarter. In Hellenic antiquity, the dark of the moon is mentioned as the suitable time for magical operations; for such, no doubt, as were concerned with a forwarding of life. Our collection exhibits the full survival of the usage and theory. It is the new moon to which is dedicated the money that under its expanding influence will be sure to multiply; it is at such time that the seed is to be put into the ground. On the contrary, the abolishment of pests and diminution of objects in which shrinkage is desired may be obtained by connecting these with the waning sphere.

Lunar change has had an important connection with ancient myth as well as with primitive ritual. For the reason indicated, the crescent was assigned as an emblem to goddesses of growth. This ornament passed from Cybele and Diana to Mary; as on the vault of St. Mark's the Virgin wears the starry robe of the earlier goddess, so on garden walls of Venice she stands crowned with the crescent, in the same manner as the divinities whom she has superseded. In this connection is especially to be considered the habit of personification implied in our English rhymes. Of late, the doctrine which perceives in myth a symbolic expression of the forces of nature has fallen into comparative discredit, a contempt explicable in view of the unscientific manner in which "sun-myths" have been exploited; our English sayings, therefore, are to be received as a welcome demonstration that one must not proceed too far in his attitude of doubt. If the popular mind, to-day, and in a country particularly accessible to the influences of modern culture, worships the personified moon, it may be considered as certain that antiquity did the like. Mythology is woven out of so many strands that goddesses like Artemis and Diana may have been much more than lunar personifications; but I think it can scarce be doubted that in a measure such they were.

(There is to be noted a most important characteristic of modern superstition, namely, that the original usage, and also the primitive theory, has sometimes continued the longest, because founded on the broadest and most human foundation.))The modern survival exhibits those fundamental conceptions out of which grew the complicated rites and elaborate mythologies of ancient religions. In this manner, as from a height of observation, we are able to look back beyond recorded history, and to trace the principles of historic development. So may be elucidated problems which neither metaphysical speculation nor historical research has proved adequate to expound. Comparative study of folk-lore has placed in our hands a key which ingenious theorists, proceeding with that imperfect knowledge of antiquity which can be gathered from books, have lacked, and for the want of which they have wandered in hopeless error.

In modern folk-belief the influence of the sun is less directly apparent. The custom of saluting the rising orb, with which the day was once begun, or of ascending high places where the benediction of the luminary could be obtained, and the direct reverence to solar rays belonging to all primitive life, survives only in the vague symbolism which, until very lately, has caused churches to be built on hills. But a single essential feature of sun-worship still survives, not only among ignorant and isolated peasants, but in the households and among the matrons of educated English-speaking folk. To this significant relic, so far as I know, Mrs. Bergen has been the first to direct attention. That the sun moves in a particular course must have been one of the first observations which primitive man made in regard to the movements of celestial bodies. His cardinal rule being to perform everything decently and in order, it followed that the precedent set in heaven was to be imitated on earth. In any operation for which success must be sought, progress must be sun-wise; the reverse order could be suitable only for operations of destructive magic, tending to undo natural sequences. Nevertheless, even primitive man has a passion for originality, a desire to obtain peculiarly intimate relations with nature, which may be to the advantage of his own people; probably from this consideration certain American tribes have reversed the ceremonial order, so far at least as to make their processional movements in the opposite direction; but our modern customs or household life show, among the ancestors of English folk, that the sun-wise circuit entered not only into the religious life, but also mingled with and directed the most ordinary actions. Little does the modern housewife, who in beating the egg instinctively stirs her spoon in one direction, — a form of movement usually recommended by no conscious association of ideas, — imagine that in the method of her action she is bearing testimony to the deepest ethical and ceremonial conceptions of remote ancestors; yet there can be no doubt that such is the case. Here also prevails the remarkable principle to which attention has already been directed. The mythology of the ancient worship has perished, but the notion which inspired the ritual practice has survived; sun-worship is thus shown to have been characteristic of our forefathers, as indeed, in all probability, it was an original feature of primitive human life. In this case, also, could we go back a little way in time, we should probably find a conception of the sun as a personal being united with usages arising from contemplation of this path.

It is always found that especial conservatism attaches to customs and ideas associated with death; the disinclination to exercise independent thought on a subject so serious leaves the field open for the continuance of ancestral notions and practices. It is therefore natural that the volume of superstition associated with the end of life should only be paralleled by that connected with the marriage relation. A vast number of actions and experiences still pass as the "signs" of approaching departure. As in omens generally, the prevailing principle is usually the effect of association of ideas; the shock to the nerves consequent on the imagination of the occurrence is, in the popular fancy, inseparable from belief in its reality. Hence the general tendency to insist on euphemistic speech, the required abstinence from unpleasant suggestions, the *favete linguis* of the Roman. In this body of deeds to be avoided, ancient and modern notions are interwoven. One must not pass under a ladder, for a ladder is used in modern executions; (one must not carry a spade through the house, for with a spade is dug a grave.) More in accordance with fundamentally human ideas, the delicate rose of fall presages the untimely waning of a youthful life. As with all superstition, the sign is not merely the prediction of an event; it is felt that as the avoidance of the omen would be to escape its consequence, so the careless action, in becoming the presage of calamity, is likewise its cause. Here appear natural antinomies of human thought: on the one hand, the sense of the inevitableness of the designated fate; on the other hand, the consciousness of ability by altering conditions to change conclusions. Thus the thoughts and actions of primitive man are inspired by the same contending intellectual forces which in later time appear under the guise of warring philosophies.

Still more remarkable are the remains of world-old usage, wherein may be remarked tendencies which have formerly been expressed in elaborate rituals. In customs relating to death, a controlling feature is that sense of individual possession which has been prevalent from a time antecedent to the rudimentary beginnings of civilization. To early man, doubt is but a change of state; the head of the household, in his place, be it the tumulus erected for his shelter, be it the distant land to which his spirit has been transported, holds the same rights and is entitled to the same privileges which on earth he enjoyed. His wives, his slaves, his steeds, his arms, are his own, property, which none dare meddle with, inasmuch as the departed, now more than heretofore, has the power to enforce his title. In a measure, therefore, these possessions must accompany him on his voyage, and remain with him in his new abode. But this deprivation is too great: in the natural course of things, the living cannot waive so much and continue to live. A part is given for the whole; substitution takes the place of direct offering. The dead is no more to be received among the living, bringing with him, as he does, a claim on other lives; by many methods, by concealment, placation, substitution, ritual exile, he must be banned to the place where only on occasions he may be sought and consulted. One of these methods of avoidance is the habit of making the return of the funeral procession so intricate that the spirit may be deceived in its attempt to retrace the route; it is perhaps a consequence of this manner of thought that even now, in retired districts, it is held unwise for the mourners to return on the same path by which they proceeded.

These usages change their character, inasmuch as the original intent of ceremonial actions being forgotten, acts intended to secure more practical ends are performed in order to correspond to supposed obligations of decency. Such is the case with the arrangement of the chamber of death, with the stoppage of the clock, of which traces are found in customary usage; so it is with the inversion of garments, of which also in our lore traces seem to linger. Different, perhaps, is the idea underlying the covering of the mirror; indications show that the practice was once extended to all objects in the room, which formerly seems to have been draped with white cloth. The object appears to have been to protect domestic objects from the contamination caused by contact with the dead, which would protect them from subsequent employment by the living, who otherwise could not with safety associate themselves with the other world just as even at the present time it is not held lucky to wear the garments of the departed. In the same manner the Mosaic law commanded the Israelite to cover, at the time of death, the vessels used in his tent. It has been remarked that white, and not black, is the proper color for such drapery. The association of white with the dead, as the hue of mourning, is ancient; it appears to me that the idea of ritual purity, expressed by the color, is at the bottom of the custom. In Hellenic times white continued to be the hue most

closely associated with the dead, albeit black, as the sign of melan-
choly, was also introduced. The character of funeral rites, from
Western Europe to Japan, exhibits a similarity which, in my judgment, is to be explained only on the supposition of very early and
long continued historical contact, — a contact otherwise demon-
strable.

On the other hand, a world-old custom, which may be set down
as human and universal, dictated, and among all nomadic peoples
continues to dictate, the abandonment of any habitation in which
a death has occurred. The obvious motive is expressed in a surviving superstition that a second decease is likely to follow a first.
Death, naturally impersonated and identified with the spirit of the
departed, will return to the place where he has once made himself
at home, and in which he has proprietary rights. This idea consti-
tutes a superstition which stands directly in the way of progress ;
thus the Navajo refuses to build a house, which at the first mor-
tality among his family it would be necessary to desert. The cause
of the general custom is to be sought, not in any sanitary principle,
but in the associations explained, acting with superstitious force.
In the course of time and with the advance of culture such deser-
tion is no longer possible, and some means must be found by which
the requirement shall be evaded ; the desired escape is effected by
such alterations as shall vary the character of the mansion and indicate it as a new place of abode, not subject to the perils of the home
invaded by death.

The remarks which have been offered are presented only by way
of suggestions which could be indefinitely extended. To construct
a commentary on the body of beliefs presented in this volume would
be an enticing but a laborious task ; such notes, also, would far
exceed in volume the compass of this work. Besides, as originally
remarked, the present collection contains but a part of the volume
of surviving superstitions. For these reasons, it will be possible to
proceed no farther.

In commending this collection to the attention of psychologists,
and to the continuing industry of students of folk-lore, I need only
express my hope that it may be sufficient to make clear how far-
reaching are the studies for which folk-lore supplies material. The
history of religion, the theory of mythologies, cannot afford to over-
look modern popular beliefs, in which ancient conceptions appear as
still effective. In the same way, archæology, regarded only as the
investigation of monuments and literatures, and dissociated from
the observation of continuing human life, is devoid of inspiration
and vitality. These studies, when accompanied with disregard of
the existing world, and indifference to the fortunes and relations of

humanity as a whole, remain not only incomplete, but positively misleading, and devoid of their best claim on respect and attention. It is to be hoped that this interesting collection, made under so many difficulties, will have a useful effect in helping to emphasize this truth, and to render obvious the possible uses of traditional information.

CAMBRIDGE, MASS., Dec. 24, 1895.

CURRENT SUPERSTITIONS.

CHAPTER I.

BABYHOOD.

1. THE bairn that is born on fair Sunday
Is bonny and loving, and blithe and gay.
Monday's bairn is fair in the face,
Tuesday's bairn is full of grace,
Wednesday's bairn is loving and giving,
Thursday's bairn works hard for a living,
Friday's bairn is a child of woe,
Saturday's bairn has far to go.

Massachusetts.

2. Monday's child is fair of face,
Tuesday's child is full of grace,
Wednesday's child is sour and sad,
Thursday's child is merry and glad,
Friday's child is loving and giving,
Saturday's child must work for a living ;
But the child that is born on the Sabbath day
Is blithe and bonny, good and gay.

Baldwinsville, N. Y.

(Some put it, Sunday's child shall never know want.)

3. He who is born on New Year's morn
Will have his own way as sure as you 're born.

4. He who is born on an Easter morn
Shall never know want, or care, or harm.

5. A child born on a saint's day must bear the saint's name. It is unlucky to take away the day from it.   *Catholic superstition.*

6. Thursday has one lucky hour, just before sunrise, for birth.

BAPTISM.

7. If a child cries during baptism, it is the devil going out of it.
Niagara Falls, Ont.

16. A child born with a veil over its face will never be drowned. Many sailors are known to wear the caul, with which they were born, about the person as a charm against death by drowning.

Sailor's superstition.

INTRODUCTION TO THE WORLD.

17. Take the baby first into the sunlight on Sunday. Put it into short clothes and make all changes on that day.

18. To make a child rise in the world, carry it upstairs (or to the attic) first. *Mifflintown, Pa.*

19. The baby must go upstairs before it goes downstairs, or it will never rise in the world. *Massachusetts.*

20. To be a bright baby, it must go up before it is carried down, and it must be bumped to the attic roof for luck.

New England.

21. A young baby was taken up a short step-ladder by its nurse

CHAPTER I.

BABYHOOD.

1. THE bairn that is born on fair Sunday
    Is bonny and loving, and blithe and gay.
    Monday's bairn is fair in the face,
    Tuesday's bairn is full of grace,
    Wednesday's bairn is loving and giving,
    Thursday's bairn works hard for a living,
    Friday's bairn is a child of woe,
    Saturday's bairn has far to go.
                                        Massachusetts.

2. Monday's child is fair of face,
    Tuesday's child is full of grace,
    Wednesday's child is sour and sad,
    Thursday's child is merry and glad,
    Friday's child is loving and giving,
    Saturday's child must work for a living ;
                    the Sabbath day

28. A child's tumbling out of bed is a sign he will never be a fool.
                                        Maine.

29. To drink water out of a bucket which is being carried on a child's head stops its growth.   *Virginia.*

30. To step over a young child stops its growing.   *Virginia.*

31. About 1860 the Alabama negresses believed that if any one stepped on their pickaninnies it would dwarf them.

32. Pass a baby through a window and it will never grow.
                                        South Carolina.

33. Do not go for the first time into the room where the infant is without removing the veil and gloves.

34. If the "cradle cap" of a baby be combed with a (fine ?) tooth comb, the child will be blind.   *Labrador.*

35. A baby should not look into a glass before it is a year old ; if it does it will die.   *Deer Isle, Me.*

36. Hold a baby to a looking-glass, he will die before he completes his first year. *Massachusetts.*

37. If you let a child look into a looking-glass before it is a year old, it will cut its teeth hard.
Baltimore, Md. (negro), and Virginia.

38. It is bad luck not to weigh the baby before it is dressed. When it is first dressed put the clothes on over the feet instead of the head for good luck.

39. The common nurse has an objection to weighing a new-born baby.

40. Always give a baby salt before it tastes aught else. The child will not choke, and in general it is a good thing to do.
Mansfield, O.

FIRST ACTIONS.

41. If a child cries at birth and lifts up one hand, he is born to command.

42. If the baby smiles in its sleep, it is talking with angels.

43. If a baby yawns, the sign of the cross should be made over it that the evil spirit may not enter. *Niagara Falls, Ont.*

44. While tying on a baby's cap repeat, —

> Look up there and see a fly,
> Look down there and see it die.

Its chin will follow the direction indicated, and the tying is hastened. *Brookline, Mass.*

VARIOUS.

45. First a daughter, then a son,
> The world is well begun.
> First a son, then a daughter,
> Trouble follows after.
Maine and Massachusetts.

46. First a son, then a daughter,
> You 've begun just as you oughter.
Brookline, Mass.

47. Rock a cradle empty,
> Babies will be plenty.
Peabody, Mass.

48. Rock the cradle empty,
Have children a plenty,
Rock the chair empty,
Have sickness a plenty.
Nashua, N. H.

49. To rock the cradle when the baby is not in it will kill it.
New York.

50. If the empty cradle be rocked, the baby will have the colic.
New York and Ohio.

51. The first time a baby is taken visiting, if it is laid on a married couple's bed there will be a baby for that couple.
Salem, Mass.

52. The mother who gives away all the clothes of her dead baby will eventually be comforted by the coming of another child.

53. However many children a woman may have, the last will be of the same gender as the first, and they will look alike.
Maine and Massachusetts.

54. One article of an unborn infant's wardrobe must be left unmade or unbought or the child is liable not to live.
Salem, Mass.

55. A baby's nails must not be cut with scissors before it is a year old; it will make it steal. *North Carolina.*

56. To cut a baby's finger-nails deforms it; if the baby is a month old, to do this will cause the child to have fits. *Georgia.*

57. To allow a child to look into a mirror before it is a month old will cause it trouble in teething. *Georgia.*

58. Tickling a baby causes stuttering. *Georgia.*

59. If an infant be measured, it will die before its growing time is over. *Georgia.*

CHAPTER II.

CHILDHOOD.

ASSEVERATION.

60. A CHILD to whom is told any story which he considers remarkable will usually reply by an expression of skepticism, such as: "Really and truly?" "Honestly?" "Earnest, now?" or, "You are fooling." The first speaker answers by some formula or asseveration, as, "Honor bright" (*New England*); "Deed, deed, and double deed" (*Pennsylvania*); "True as I live," or, "Hope I'll die if it is n't so," or simply, "Hope I'll die."

General in the United States.

61. A formula of asseveration in Maryland and Pennsylvania is, "I cross my heart," accompanied by the sign of the cross.

62. A sign resembling that of the cross is made on the chin or throat. "You won't tell?" "No." "Well, cross your throat."

Cambridge, Mass.

63. When a child wishes to make an asseveration, he wets his finger on his mouth and signs a cross on his throat.

Salem, Mass.

64. In asseveration, the proper method is to use the words, "Hope to die if I don't," the speaker drawing the forefinger across the throat from ear to ear. *Biddeford, Me.*

65. Asseveration in Maine and Massachusetts is often made by the following formula. First boy: "Honor bright?" Second boy: "Hope to die." First boy: "Cut your throat?" Second boy draws finger across throat. This is the strongest possible form of oath that can be taken by a boy.

66. Little girls, without any idea of the meaning, employ the following formula of asseveration : —

Certain, true,
Black and blue.

A variant of the first line : "Certain and true."

Massachusetts.

67. A form fuller than the preceding : —

> Certain, true,
> Black and blue,
> Lay me down and cut me in two.

68. A boy who desires to tell an extravagant story without being guilty of a lie would point with his thumb over his left shoulder. If he should succeed in accomplishing this without the observation of the boy to whom he is talking, so much the better.

Biddeford, Me.

69. "In my school-days, if a boy crossed his fingers, elbows, and legs, though the act might not be noticed by the companion accosted, no blame was attached to the falsehood."

New York city.

70. The addition of the words "in a horn" justify a falsehood. In the childhood of the informant, it was not considered honorable to express the words in such manner that they could not be heard by the child with whom conversation was carried on.

Cambridge, Mass.

71. In making a false statement, it was proper to say "over the left." This was often uttered in such manner that the person addressed should not perceive the qualification. Or, the statement would be made, and after it had been taken in and believed, the words "over the left" would be added.

Ohio and Cambridge, Mass.

72. A formula for making a false statement : "As true as I lie here," said, as one fools, gives free scope to white lies.

Roxbury, Mass.

73. An imprecation of children against disloyalty : —

> Tell tale tit,
> Your tongue shall be slit,
> And every dog in our town
> It shall have a bit.

Ohio.

CHALLENGE.

To "stump" another boy to do a thing is considered as putting a certain obligation on him to perform the action indicated. The phrase is sometimes used, although the person giving the "stump" may not himself be able to accomplish the feat.

74. We used to "dare" or "stump" one another to eat green "chuckcherries."

Brookline, Mass.

75. Daring or "stumping" is or has been common among children generally. Sometimes it is to jump a certain distance; sometimes to skate out on thin ice; again, to touch something very hot. Once in Ohio several lads were collected together about a spring. One of them drew a pail of fresh water and by chance brought up a small live fish. One of the boys "stumped" his companions to eat the fish alive, without dressing or cooking. The boys took the "stump," one quickly cut up the unfortunate little animal and each boy swallowed a bit. Often the dare is to eat some very untoothsome morsel.

FORTUNE.

76. Put a mark upon a paper for every bow you get, and when you have one hundred bury the paper and wish. When the paper is decayed you will find your wish in its place.

Cambridge and Bedford, Mass.

77. Children collect two or three hundred names of persons, asking each to give a bow with the name. This bow is expressed after the name on a sheet of paper on which the latter is written by this sign *N*. After all are collected the paper is secretly buried face downward, and then dug up after two or three months, when money is sometimes found under it.

North Cambridge, Mass.

78. At Christmas or New Year's children, on first meeting, call out " My Christmas-gift," or " New Year's-gift," and the one who calls first is to receive a gift from the other. *Mansfield, O.*

FRIENDSHIP.

79. If two persons, while walking, divide so as to pass an obstruction one on one side and one on the other, they will quarrel. Children avert this catastrophe by exclaiming, "bread and butter," which is a counter charm. On the other hand, if they say "pepper and salt," the quarrel is made doubly certain. So universal is the practice that many grown people of the best social class (women) still involuntarily avoid such separation, and even use the childish words. In country towns, when girls are walking with young men, if the latter pass on the other side of the tree it is considered as rude, and as a token of indifference; in such a case one girl will cast a meaning look on her companion as much as to say, " he does not care for you." To use the local phrase, it would be said, So-and-so is "mad" with —— (naming the girl). *Massachusetts.*

80. In passing a tree in the middle of the sidewalk, children used

to pass it on one side going one way and on the other side going the other way for luck. *Billerica, Mass.*

MYTHOLOGY.

81. The stars are angels' eyes. *Westminster, Mass.*

82. (The stars are holes made in the sky, so that the light of heaven shines through.) "I remember, as a child, that this idea was suggested to me on seeing the effect of holes in the lamp shade. I think, however, that I rather liked to suppose it true and firmly believed in the explanation." *Cambridge, Mass.*

83. "As a child, I constantly looked into lilies and tulips in the expectation of finding fairies lying within them." *Mansfield, O.*

84. "I remember that as a child, while walking with a companion, she cried : 'Why, a fairy lighted on my hand!' The child believed that this had been the case." *Cambridge, Mass.*

85. The children used to fearfully look in the well, and on seeing the reflected face in the bottom, would cry out, "Face in the well, pull me down in the well," and would then run away quickly. *Bruynswick, N. Y.*

86. At the age of six or seven years, a child, while going to a spring to draw water, saw a little creature with wings fly from one star to another, leaving behind an arc of light. She cried to her aunt : "Oh, aunt, I saw a little gold-boy!" Her aunt, somewhat shocked, rebuked the child, who insisted on the literal truth of her vision. *Mansfield, O.*

87. Stick your thumb through a knothole and say : —

> Old Gran'f'ther Graybeard, without tooths or tongue,
> If you 'll give me a little finger I 'll give you a thumb.
> Thumb 'll go away and little finger 'll come.

88. Go to the woodpile and say, " Johnnie with your fingers, and Willie with your toes," and something (suthin) will come out of the woodpile and tear off all your clothes (close). *Gilsum, N. H.*

PUNISHMENT.

89. An "eyewinker" placed in the palm of the hand will cause the ferule to break when the teacher strikes the palm with it. *Portsmouth, N. H.*

90. Pine tar or pitch in the hand will prevent the blows of the ferule from causing pain. (*Portsmouth, N. H.*, sixty years ago.) Believed by most schoolboys there at that time.

SPORT.

91. At croquet, if your ball was about to be sent flying, the safeguard was to draw an imaginary X with your mallet, saying, "Criss cross." It made your enemy's foot slip, and many a girl would get "mad" and not play, if you did it often.   *Brookline, Mass.*

92. Children believe it is unlucky to step on the cracks in the flagstones, which are believed to contain poison. It is a game to walk a long distance on such stones without setting foot on the interstices.   *Cambridge, Mass.*

93. When children are tired of swinging, or think it is time for the swinger to give way to another, the phrase is "let the old cat die." After this has been said, it is unlucky to quicken the motion of the swing again.   *General.*

VARIOUS.

94. When a child loses a tooth, if the tongue is not put into the cavity a gold tooth will come in place of it.
                New York and Northern Ohio.

95. The ideas of children about the significance of color are mixed. Thus in croquet no child (in a town near Boston) would take the red ball, because it was supposed to mean hate. Blue is the favorite color.

96. Red and yellow, catch a fellow.   *Brookline, Mass.*
Pink and blue, he 'll catch you.   *Deerfield, Mass.*
Pink and blue, he 'll be true.   *Deerfield, Mass.*
Black and white, hold him tight.   *Pennsylvania.*

97. An old superstition which still survives among children is, that if they crawl over an older person and do not crawl back they will never grow again.   *Haverhill, Mass.*

98. "We used always as children to get X's scored with a pin on our new 'village gaiters.' We were told it was to make them safe and take the slipperiness off."   *Brookline, Mass.*

99. Children say that the one who takes the first bite of an apple that is to be passed about for eating will fail in his or her lesson.

Chelsea, Mass.

100. Boys believe that they can prevent the stitch in the side which is liable to be induced by running, by means of holding a pebble under the tongue. " I believe I could run all day, and not get tired, if I could hold a pebble under my tongue," said one.

Cambridge, Mass.

CHAPTER III.

PHYSICAL CHARACTERISTICS.

BEAUTY.

101. IF a person is very handsome, it is a sign that he will have one of the infectious diseases of childhood (measles, whooping cough, etc.) more than once. *Massachusetts.*

DIMPLE.

102. Dimple in chin,
Devil within.
Chestertown, Md.

103. A dimple in the chin is lucky. Some say "it shows you're no fool."

104. A dimple is the mark left by the angel's finger in turning up the face to kiss it when asleep. *Pennsylvania.*

EARS.

105. Small ears indicate that a person is stingy. Large ones show that he is generous. *General.*

106. Large ears are a mark of a liar. Small ears show that one is truthful. *Boston, Mass.*

107. Long, slim ears are a sign that you will steal.
Chestertown, Md.

108. If the protuberance behind the ear is large, it indicates generosity. *Massachusetts.*

EYES AND EYEBROWS.

109. Hazel eyes betoken a good disposition. *Boston, Mass.*

110. If your eyebrows meet, you will be rich.
Somerville and Bedford, Mass.

111. A well-known children's rhyme runs : —

> Blue-eye beauty, do your mammy's duty !
> Black eye, pick a pie,
> Run around and tell a lie !
> Gray-eye greedy gut
> Eat all the world up !
>
> *General in the United States.*

112. If the eyebrows meet, one is ill-tempered.

General in the United States.

113. If the eyebrows are far apart, you will live away from home; if near together, you will live near home, or at home.

Massachusetts.

114. Heavy eyebrows are a sign of long life.

Lawrence, Mass.

FINGER-NAILS.

115. Always keep your nails clean and you will be rich.

Peabody, Mass.

116. A white spot in the nail, when it comes, means a present. You get the present when it grows to the end and is cut.

Boston, Mass.

117. White spots on the nails of the left hand denote the number of lies one has told.   *Maine and Central Illinois.*

118. Count on finger-nail spots : —

> Friends,
> Foes,
> Money,
> Beaux.

Begin with the first nail spotted, and the noun falling to the last nail thus marked gives the sign.   *Deerfield, Mass.*

119. Another formula : —

> (First finger) a friend,
> (Second finger) a foe,
> (Third finger) a gift,
> (Fourth finger) a beau,
> (Fifth finger) a journey to go.
>
> *Mansfield, O.*

An almost identical variant is found in Prince Edward Island.

FOOT.

120. If your instep is high enough to have water flow under it, you are of good descent. *Brookline, Mass.*

121. A mole on the sole of the left foot means trouble and hardships during life. *Boston, Mass.*

FOREHEAD.

122. If there is a blue vein in the child's forehead extending down upon the nose, it is one of the surest signs of early death.
Maine and Massachusetts.

123. Vertical wrinkles in the brow show the number of husbands one will have. Horizontal ones show the number of children.
Northern Ohio.

HAIR.

124. Coarse hair indicates good nature ; fine hair quick temper.
Northern Ohio.

125. Red hair indicates a " spit-fire."
Massachusetts and Chestertown, Md.

126. Beware of that man,
Be he friend or brother,
Whose hair is one color
And moustache another.
Portland, Me.

127. The color of the hair growing on the neck indicates the color of the hair of one's future husband.

128. A single white hair means genius; it must not be pulled out.

129. If you pull out a white hair, two will come in its place.
Somewhat general in the United States.

130. Hair growing upon the upper lip of a woman means riches.
Boston, Mass.

131. The point formed by the hair growing on the forehead is called " A widow's peak." *Eastern Massachusetts.*

132. When a woman's hair parts where it should not, it is a sure sign she will be a widow. *Springfield, Mass.*

133. Draw a single hair from the head strongly between the thumb and finger-nail. If it curls up, you are proud.
St. John, N. B., and Prince Edward Island.

The same result indicates that you are cross. *Cape Breton.*

134. Hairy arms mean wealth. *Northern Ohio.*

135. Hairy arms mean strength.
General in the United States.

136. Scrape the finger-nail and the thumb-nail along a hair, and if, by the third time, it curls up, the owner is high-tempered.
Boston, Mass.

137. Put some of your hair in the fire. If it burns slowly you will have a long life. If quickly, a short one.
Chestertown, Md.

HAND.

138. A straight line in the palm of the hand is an omen of early death. *Massachusetts.*

139. The letter formed by the veins on the inside of the wrist is the initial of the name of the future husband or wife.
St. John, N. B.

140. A person with an initial in his hand will be very fortunate in selecting a companion for life. *Alabama.*

141. In clasping your own hand, you put uppermost either your right or your left thumb. If the former, you are to rule; *vice versa,* you yield. *Brookline, Mass.*

142. If the thumb sticks up in the closed fist, you are either capable or honest, probably the latter, as thieves are said to double theirs in.
New England.

143. If you cannot make your thumb and one finger meet around your wrist, you are a glutton. *Province of Quebec.*

144. If you cannot touch the tips of your little finger and first finger together behind the two middle fingers, on both hands, then you will not marry the man you want to marry.
Province of Quebec.

145. Clasp your fingers, and if the right thumb lap over the left you were born in the daytime. If the left overlap, you were born at night.

146. The number of folds on your wrist as you bend your hand shows the number of thirties you are to live. *Massachusetts.*

147. If the ends of the fingers are capable of being bent far back, it indicates a thief.

MOLES.

148. A mole on the eyebrow denotes that one will be hanged. On the ear it denotes that he will be drowned.

Chestertown, Md.

149. Mole above breath
Means wealth.

150. Moles on the neck,
Money by the peck.
Prince Edward Island and Northern Ohio.

151. A mole on the neck indicates that its owner will be hanged.
Boston, Mass.

152. A mole on the side of the neck means a death by hanging.
Central Maine.

153. A mole on the arm indicates riches.   *Boston, Mass.*

154. Mole on your arm,
Live on a farm.
Alabama.

155. A mole on the arm means that you will fight many battles, and will be very successful in them.   *Prince Edward Island.*

NOSE.

156. A vein across the nose is an omen of short life.
General in the United States.

TEETH.

157. A broad space between the teeth indicates a liar.
Biddeford, Me.

158. Broad front teeth mean that one is generous.
Biddeford, Me.

159. A space between the two front upper incisors signifies wealth.   *Mansfield, O.*

160. If the front teeth are wide apart, it means one can't keep a secret.   If overlapping, one is close-mouthed.   *Boston, Mass.*

161. Do not trust people with pointed teeth.
Chestertown, Md.

162. If you have a space between your teeth, it is a sign that you will die of consumption.   *Baltimore, Md.*

163. A lump (enlarged papilla) on the tongue is a sign one has told a lie.   *Mansfield, O.*

CHAPTER IV.

PROJECTS.

LOVE divinations or love charms, I have found, are popularly known as "projects" in parts of New England and on Mt. Desert. On Prince Edward Island and in various parts of the Canadian provinces the practice of such divinations is usually spoken of as "trying tricks." If a number of young people are together, one will say, "Let's try tricks." In the Middle and Western United States the usual colloquial expression for these love divinations is "trying fortunes." One girl will say to another at some appropriate time, "Let's try our fortunes."

APPLES.

164. Eat an apple at midnight before the glass, saying, —

> Whoever my true love may be,
> Come and eat this apple with me,

holding the lamp in the hand. The true love will appear.

Winn, Me.

165. Throw a whole apple-paring on the floor, after swinging it three times around your head. It will form your true love's initial letter. *General in the United States.*

APPLE-SEEDS.

166. When eating an apple, snap it with the fingers and name it for a person of the opposite sex. Count the fully developed seeds (all of the others are kisses), and the last one must correspond to the following formula : —

> One 's my love,
> Two 's my love,
> Three 's my heart's desire.
> Four I 'll take and never forsake,
> Five I 'll cast in the fire.
> Six he loves,
> Seven she loves,
> Eight they both love,

Nine he comes,
Ten he tarries,
Eleven he goes,
Twelve he marries.
Thirteen honor,
Fourteen riches,
All the rest are little witches.

Baldwinsville, N. Y.

Some change the latter lines of this formula into

Thirteen they quarrel,
Fourteen they part,
Fifteen they die with a broken heart.

167. Similar rhymes commonly repeated in northern Ohio, after naming an apple and counting the seeds, are, —

One I love,
Two I love,
Three I love, I say.
Four I love with all my heart,
And five I cast away.
Six he loves,
Seven she loves,
Eight they both love.
Nine he comes,
Ten he tarries,
Eleven he courts,
And twelve he marries.

Prince Edward Island and Mansfield, O.

168. Lay in the hand four apple-seeds and have some one name them, then pick them up, saying, —

This one I love all others above,
And this one I greatly admire,
And this one I 'll take and never forsake.
And this one I 'll cast in the fire.

St. John, N. B.

169. A love divination by way of apple-seeds, much practiced when a number of young people were spending the evening together, or perhaps by grown-up boys and girls in district schools as they ate their noon-day lunch about the stove, was as follows : —

Two seeds were named, one for a girl and one for a young man, and placed on a hot stove or in front of an open fire. The augury, concerning the future relations of the young people was derived from the behavior of the two seeds. If as they heated they jumped away from one another, the two persons would become estranged or their friendship die ; if the seeds moved nearer together, marriage was implied; if the one named for the girl moved towards the other, it signified that the young woman was fonder of the young man than he was of her, and so on. *Northern Ohio.*

170. "A common project in my girlhood was to place an apple-seed on each of the four fingers of the right hand, that is, on the knuckles, first moistening them with spittle. A companion then 'named' them, and the fingers were worked so as to move slightly. The seed that stayed on the longest indicated the name of your future husband." *Stratham, N. H.*

171. Name apple-seeds and place on the lids of. the closed eyes. Wink and the first to fall off shows the name of your future husband. *Winn, Me., New York, and Pennsylvania.*

172. To name apple-seeds, put one on each temple, get some one to name them, and the one that sticks the longest will be the true one.

173. Name apple pips, put them on the grate, saying, —

If you love me, live and fly ;
If you do not, lie and die.

BABIES.

174. Kiss the baby when nine days old, and the first gentleman you kiss afterward will be your future husband. *New England.*

BED.

175. Go upstairs backward, into a chamber backward, and into bed backward. Drink some salt and water, and if you dream of some one bringing you drink it will be your future husband. *Maine and Salem, Mass.*

176. The first time two girls sleep together let them tie two of their big toes together with woollen yarn, and the one with the shortest piece of broken string left attached in the morning will be married first. *Northern Ohio.*

177. If two girls on sleeping together for the first time tie their waists together with string or thread, and the thread gets broken in the night, the first man who puts his arm round the waist of either

will have the first name of the man whom that girl will marry, whether that man is the one or not. *Province of Quebec.*

178. After getting ready for bed in silence, take a ball of string and wind about the wrist, repeating, —

> I wind, I wind,
> This night to find,
> Who my true love's to be ;
> The color of his eyes,
> The color of his hair,
> And the night he 'll be married to me.

Chestertown, Md.

179. Name the bed-posts for four different men. The one you dream about you will marry. *General.*

180. The first time you sleep in a room name the corners each with a different (man's) name. The first corner you face on waking indicates whom you will marry. (*New England.*) The same thing is done with the bed-posts in Ohio.

181. Put four names of boys on four slips of paper and take one blank slip. Intermingle them, and then without looking at them put one under each leg of the bed and one under the pillow. The name of the last will be that of your future husband.

Franklin, Mass.

182. Rub the four bed-posts with a lemon and carry the lemon in the pocket the next day, and the first man you speak to you will marry. *New Hampshire.*

BIBLE.

183. Read the third verse of the third chapter of Hosea, Joel, and Amos for three Sundays in succession, and the first gentleman you walk with you will marry. *Nashua, N. H.*

184. Put the end of a key in the Bible, on the verse of Solomon's Song reading, " I am my beloved's and he is mine ; " close the book and bind it round with string or garter, each girl supporting the key with the first finger of the right hand. One of them repeats a verse to each letter as the other girl names it, beginning the alphabet, till it turns at the initial of the future husband or lover.

General in the United States.

BIRDS.

185. When you see a turkey-buzzard flying alone, repeat, —

> Hail! Hail! Lonely, lonesome turkey-buzzard :
> Hail to the East, hail to the West,
> Hail to the one that I love best.
> Let me know by the flap of your wing
> Whether he (or she) loves me or not.

Note the manner of the bird's flight: if he flaps his wings your lover is true ; if not, the lover is false. *Tennessee.*

186. When the call of the first turtle-dove is heard, sit down and remove the shoe and stocking from the left foot, turn the stocking inside out, in the heel of which if a hair is found, it will be of the color of the hair of the future husband or wife. *Tennessee.*

In Mt. Desert, Maine, and Prince Edward Island the same project is tried on hearing the first robin.

BUTTONS.

187. The coming husband is determined by repeating the following words, touching each button of the coat, vest, or dress in order : —

> Rich man, poor man, beggar man, thief,
> Doctor, lawyer, Indian chief.

Or,

> Doctor, lawyer, merchant, chief.

Or,

> Doctor, lawyer, merchant, cheat. *Ohio.*

188. With reference to the habitation to be occupied : —

> Big house, little house, pig-sty, barn.
> *New Hampshire.*

189. As to the wedding dress : —

> Silk, satin, velvet, cotton, woolen. *Massachusetts.*

190. In regard to the vehicle : —

> Carriage, wagon, wheelbarrow, chaise.
> *Massachusetts.*

191. The first of these button formulæ is used by boys to foretell their profession in life. A friend remembers how in childhood his buttons were completely worn out by the continual practice of the inquiry.

192. With reference to the acquisition of a coat : —
Bought, given, stolen. *Massachusetts.*

193. "Rich man, poor man, beggar, thief, doctor, lawyer, merchant, chief." Said over by little girls on their back hair combs to find the occupation of their future husbands. *New York.*

FOUR-LEAVED CLOVER.

194. If a girl puts a two-leaved clover in her shoe, the first man who comes on the side where the clover is will be her future husband. *Michigan.*

195. Put a four-leaved clover in your shoe, and you will marry a man having the first name of the man whom you meet first after doing it. *Province of Quebec.*

196. With a four-leaved clover in your shoe, you will meet your lover. *Michigan.*

197. If the finder of a four-leaved clover put it in her own shoe, she will marry the first person with whom she crosses a bridge. *Michigan.*

198. Put a four-leaved clover over the door. The first person to pass beneath will be your future mate.
Newport, R. I., and Michigan.

COUNTING.

199. Count sixty white horses and one white mule, then you will marry the first man with whom you shake hands.
Chestertown, Md.

200. Count a hundred white horses and two white mules, and the first person you shake hands with you 'll marry. *Pennsylvania.*

201. Count a hundred white horses during leap year. The first man that shakes hands with you after you have your hundred will be your future husband. *Bedford, Mass.*

202. Count one hundred gray horses (one mule stands for ten horses), and the first gentleman with whom you shake hands is your intended. *Alabama.*

203. After meeting ninety-nine white horses and a brown one for

the hundredth, the first person with whom you shake hands will be your future mate. *Newport, R. I.*

204. Count five hundred colored people, and the next gentleman you meet you will marry. *Cambridge, Mass.*

205. Count ninety-nine negroes and one white horse, and the first boy you answer " yes " or " no " to you will marry. *South Boston, Mass.*

206. Count forty white horses, the first man you meet afterwards you'll marry. *Champaign, Ill.*

207. In crossing a bridge, if one sees two white horses on it (in different teams) and wishes at once for a man to marry her, she'll get him. *Peabody, Mass.*

208. Count a hundred "tips" (a bow with the lifting of the hat). The hundredth will be your future husband. *Eastern Massachusetts.*

209. Count the buttons of an old boot. The number of buttons indicates the number of years before marriage. *Massachusetts.*

210. If you count the boards of the ceiling (loft) in a strange room before going to sleep, you will dream of your lover. *Newfoundland.*

DAISY PETALS.

211. Pull off the "petals" of a daisy one by one, naming a boy (or a girl as the case may be) at each one, thus, " Jenny, Fanny, Jenny, Fanny," etc. The one named with the last petal is your sweetheart. The seeds which remain on the back of your hand after taking them up show the number of your children.

212. Common at the present time is the formula : —
He loves me, he loves me not.

213. To tell the fortune, take an "ox-eye daisy," and pluck the "petals" one by one, using the same words as have been given above for buttons. *General in the United States.*

In Ohio and other Western States where the ox-eye daisy is not common, children use instead the bloom of the despised dog-fennel.

214. Fortunes are told by pulling off leaflets of a compound leaf, such as the locust, repeating, " Rich man, poor man," etc. *Central Illinois.*

215. Name a daisy, and then pull off the petals (ray-flowers) one by one, saying " yes, no," and if "yes" falls on the last, the person loves you, and *vice versa.* *Alabama.*

216. A formula for daisy petals : —

> He loves me,
> He don't ;
> He 'll have me,
> He won't ;
> He would if he could,
> But he can't.

New Brunswick.

217. If you find a five-leaf daisy (that is, one with five ray-flowers) and swallow it without chewing, you will in the course of the day shake hands with your intended. *Alabama.*

218. Another : —

> Hate her,
> Have her,
> This year,
> Next year,
> Sometime,
> Never.

New Brunswick.

219. Another : —

> He loves,
> She loves,
> Hate her,
> Have her,
> This year,
> Next year,
> Now or never.

Cape Breton.

Girls repeat the last three lines only of the above rhyme.

Prince Edward Island.

DOORWAY.

220. Put the breast-bone of a fowl over the front door, and the first one of the opposite sex that enters is to be your future companion. *Alabama.*

221. Hang over the door a corn-cob from which you have shelled all but twenty grains. The first man that enters you 'll marry.

Arlington, Mass.

222. Nail a horseshoe over the door, and the first one who enters is your true love. *Massachusetts.*

223. Hang a wishbone over the door. The first one who enters will be your lover. *Somewhat general.*

224. Two girls break a wishbone together. The one who gets the longest bit will remain longest unmarried, or, as the familiar rhyme runs, —

> Shortest to marry,
> Longest to tarry.

If the "knot" (that is, the flattened portion at the junction of the two prongs of the bone) flies away and does not stick to either prong, the two girls are to remain unmarried. Each girl puts her bit of the wishbone over a different door. The first man who enters either door is to marry the girl who has placed her bit of wishbone over the door. *Prince Edward Island.*

EGGS.

225. Take an egg to your window; break it over a knife; remember the day and date. Wish that your true love would come to you. If you go too high, he will be killed. *Nashua, N. H.*

226. Put two eggs in front of the open fire on a very windy day, and soon two men will come in with a coffin. The man at the foot will be your future husband. *Chestertown, Md. (negro).*

227. One or more girls put eggs to roast before an open fire, seating themselves in chairs before it. Each puts one egg to roast, and when her egg begins to sweat (it will sweat blood), she is to rise and turn it. At this time the one whom that projector is to marry will come in through a door or window (all of which must be left open throughout) and take her vacant chair. If she is to die before she marries, two black dogs will enter, bearing a coffin, which they will deposit on her chair. *Quaker Neck, Kent Co., Md.*

228. Boil an egg hard, take out the yolk, and fill its place with salt. Eat it before going to bed. The one you dream of as bringing you water is your future husband. *Mansfield, O.*
To be done by two girls in silence, going backward as they retire.

FINGERS.

229. Name each of the four fingers of one hand for some person of the opposite sex, then press them tightly together with the other hand ; the one that hurts the worst indicates whom you will marry.

Prince Edward Island.

GARMENTS.

230. Scatter your clothes in the four corners of the room, naming them. The man you are to marry will bring you your clothes in a dream. *Maine.*

231. The first time you sleep in a room, name the corners each a different (man's) name. The first corner you face on waking indicates whom you will marry.

The same thing is done with bed-posts in Ohio.

232. On your birthday, as you retire at night, take off your slipper or boot. Stand with your back to the door and throw it over your head. If the toe points to the door, you go out of the chamber a bride before the year is out. You must not look at the boot until the morning. *Bedford, Mass.*

233. At night before going to bed take one of your garters and tie it in a knot and hang it on the bed-post above your head. While tying repeat, —

> This knot I tie, this knot I knit,
> To see the young man I have n't seen yet.

Chestertown, Md.

234. Young girls on going to bed at night place their shoes at right angles to one another, in the form of the letter T, repeating this rhyme : —

> Hoping this night my true love to see,
> I place my shoes in the form of a T.

Northern Ohio.

235. The first time you sleep in a house, upon retiring place the shoes in the form of a T, and say over, —

> My true love by-and-by for to see,
> Be as she (or he) be,
> Bear as she (or he) may,
> The clothes she (or he) wears every day.

Boston, Mass.

236. Catch the four corners of a handkerchief up in the hand, then

let some one wishing to try her fortune draw two. If she gets two corners on the same side, she will not be married. If she gets opposite ones, she will be married.

Prince Edward Island and Chestertown, Md.

237. A rhyme on stockings and shoes : —

> Point your shoes towards the street,
> Leave your garters on your feet,
> Put your stockings on your head,
> You 'll dream of the man you are going to wed.

Eastern Massachusetts.

238. Put the chemise, inside out, on the foot of the bed and under it a board with ashes upon it ; then go to bed backwards, saying, —

> Whoever my true love may be,
> Come write his name in these ashes for me.

Winn, Me.

239. Place the heel of one shoe against the instep of the other for three nights in a row. You will dream of your future husband.

Franklin, Mass.

240. On Friday night after getting all ready for bed, roll your petticoat up, and before lying down put it under your pillow, repeating this verse : —

> This Friday night while going to bed,
> I put my petticoat under my head,
> To dream of the living and not of the dead,
> To dream of the man I am to wed,
> The color of his eyes, the color of his hair,
> The color of the clothes he is to wear,
> And the night the wedding is to be.

Rock Hall, Md.

LETTERS OF THE ALPHABET.

241. Write names on three pieces of paper, throw them up in the air (in the dark) ; feel for one, put it under the pillow, and in the morning look at it to see the name of the man you are to marry.

Salem, Mass.

242. Put pieces of paper, each bearing one letter of the alphabet, in water face down, and then place them under the bed. Those turned up in the morning are the initials of your future husband.

Prince Edward Island and Northern Ohio.

243. Write the names of several men friends, each on a slip of paper. On three successive mornings choice is made from these. If the name drawn is always the same, it is the name of your future husband. If the lot falls differently every morning, you will never be married.

244. Write two names (of possible lovers), cross out the common letters. Touch the uncrossed letters, repeating in turn, "Love, friendship, hate," and the last uncrossed letter will indicate the state of the heart.

Prince Edward Island, St. John, N. B., and Northern Ohio.

MIDNIGHT.

245. Go out at midnight and walk around a peach-tree, repeating, —

> Low for a foreigner,
> Bark for a near one,
> Crow for a farmer,
> Screek, tree, screek, if I 'm to die first.

Quaker Neck, Md.

246. Eat an apple at midnight before the glass, saying, "Whoever my true love may be, come and eat this apple with me," while holding a lamp in the hand. Your true love will appear. *Winn, Me.*

247. Set the table in silence for two at eleven o'clock P. M., with bread and butter and silver knives and forks. Two girls sit down at twelve, and say, "Whoever my true love may be, come and eat this supper with me." *Winn, Me.*

PLANTS.

248. Take beans in the hand, go out of doors and throw them against the window. The first man's name that you hear spoken is the name of the man you will marry. *Connecticut.*

249. Put three raw beans in your mouth, go out of doors, stand in front of some one's window and listen. The first man's name you hear spoken will be either that of your future husband or of the one having the same name. *Salem, Mass.*

250. If a piece of brush or brier sticks to the dress, name it. If it drops, the lover is false ; if it sticks, he is true. *Northern Ohio.*

251. Blow seeds from the dandelion until none remain, counting each puff as a letter of the alphabet ; the letter which ends the blowing is the initial of the name of the person the blower marries.

252. Rub your hands in sweet fern. The first one you shake hands with afterward is your true love.

Prince Edward Island,

253. Wear a piece of fern in the toe of your shoe, and the first person you meet you will marry. *New Hampshire.*

254. Take a live-forever leaf, squeeze it to loosen the inner and outer skin. If it makes a balloon as you blow into it, you will be married and live a long time. If it does not, you will be an old maid. *St. John, N. B.*

255. Stick a piece of live-forever up on the wall, and in whatever direction it leans, the lover will come from that quarter. *Miramichi, N. B.*

256. Take two shoots of live-forever and pin them together on the wall. If they grow towards each other, the couple will marry; if away, they will become estranged. *Nantucket, Mass., and Western Massachusetts.*

257. Break off a piece of dodder or "lovevine," twirl it round the head three times and drop it on a bush behind you. If it grows, the lover is true; if not, he is false. *Tennessee.*

258. Twist a mullein-stalk nearly off after naming it. If it lives, he or she loves you; if not, not. *Newton, Mass., and Tennessee.*

259. After proceeding as above, count the number of new shoots that spring up (if any). The number shows how many children will result from the marriage. *Greene Co., Mo.*

260. Put a pea-pod with nine peas over the door. The first one who comes under it you will marry. *New England.*

261. Pluck three thistles in bloom, cut off the purple part and put the remainder of the flower in water over night, after naming. The one that blooms out over night you will marry. *St. John, N. B., and Northern Ohio.*

262. Saturday night walk round a tall white yarrow three times, saying, —

Good evening, good evening, Mr. Yarrow.
I hope I see you well to-night,
And trust I 'll see you at meetin' to-morrow.

Then pluck the head, put it inside the dress, and sleep with it. The first person you meet with, to speak to, at church will be your husband. *Deerfield, Mass.*

RING.

263. Suspend a ring by a hair from the finger. Let it swing over a tumbler. The number of strokes against the side of the tumbler indicates the number of years of age of the future husband.

Prince Edward Island.

264. Hang a gold ring over a glass of water, from a hair, saying the name of some man. If the ring strikes the side of the glass three times you will marry him. *Willimantic, Conn.*

265. Put three saucers on the table, and walk round it blindfolded three times, then put a finger in a saucer. One saucer contains a gold ring, one soapsuds, one is empty. Repeat twice (making nine in all). If one touches the ring, she will marry an unmarried man; if the suds, she will marry a widower; if the empty one, she will be an old maid. The one touched two out of three times is the fate.

Central Maine.

266. If a piece of wedding-cake is passed through a ring and put in the left stocking, then placed under the pillow and slept on three nights running, you will dream of your lover, or he or she will come to you. *New England.*

STARS.

267. If you look at a bright star intently before retiring, you will dream of your sweetheart. *Alabama.*

268. Count nine stars for nine successive nights. (If a rainy or cloudy night intervene, the charm is broken, and the project must be begun again.) The person you dream of on the ninth night will be your future partner in life. *Prince Edward Island.*

269. Count nine stars for nine consecutive nights, and the person you dream of the last night is your intended.

Prince Edward Island and Alabama.

270. Count nine stars for nine nights in succession, and the first young gentleman with whom you shake hands is to be your future husband. *Eastern Massachusetts.*

271. For three successive nights look out of the window and name three stars. Walk to bed backward and without speaking. The one you dream of two nights out of three will be your husband.

Central Maine.

272. Have some one call a star which you have picked out, by the name of a young man. The next time you meet this man, if his

face is toward you, he loves you; if his side, he likes you; if his back, he hates you.   *Province of Quebec and Bedford, Mass.*

TEA-LEAVES.

273. After drinking tea, turn the cup upside down, whirl it round three times, set it down in the saucer, whirl again, take it up, turn right side up, and look at the grounds. If all are settled in the bottom of the cup, you will be married right off. If they stay on the side, the number of grounds will be the number of years before marriage. The fine dust in the bottom means trouble, a wish, a letter, or a journey.   *Somewhat general in the United States.*

274. Take a "beau" (a little stem) from the tea and put it in your shoe. The first man you meet you will marry.   *St. John, N. B.*

275. Sticks of tea in the teacup denote beaux. Name them, and bite them, and the hardest loves you best.   *Massachusetts.*

WALKING ABROAD.

276. Go to walk and turn back. The first man you meet you'll marry.   *Massachusetts.*

277. If you walk the length of seven rails of a railroad track, the first man that speaks to you after you get off will be your future husband.   *Bedford, Mass.*

278. Take a looking-glass and walk backwards to the wall, and you will see your future husband's picture.   *Nashua, N. H.*

279. If you walk with a gentleman (for the first time), and have on new shoes and go over a bridge, you will marry him.
     Eastern Massachusetts.

280. If a young woman walking into a strange place picks up three pebbles and puts them under her pillow, she will marry the young man she dreams of.   *Carbonear, N. F.*

281. Run three times around the house, and on the third round a vision of your husband will rise before you.   *Alabama.*

WATER.

282. Float two cambric needles on water and name them. If they float together, they 'll marry. If they float apart, they won't marry.
Petit Codiac, N. B.

283. Girls prepare basins of dirty and of clean water. If a blind-folded girl puts a stick, with which she reaches about, into the dirty water, she will marry a widower. If into clean water, she will marry a young man.
Labrador.

284. Place three basins on the floor, one containing dirty water, another clear water, and the third empty. Let the (blindfolded ?) person crawl up to them on her hands and knees. The one she touches will foretell her fate. The clear water means she is to marry a rich man, the dirty water, a poor man, and the empty basin no man at all.

285. Make ready a mirror, a lamp, a basin of water, a towel and soap. Go to bed backward, not speaking afterwards, and lie awake till midnight. If your sweetheart comes and washes, combs his hair, and looks at you, you 'll be married. If you don't see him, you 'll see your coffin. (Both sexes.)
Labrador.

286. When a pot is boiling over, put a small stick in one of the ears and name it for the one you like best. If he loves you in return, the water will cease to boil over ; if not, it will continue.
Double Creek, Md.

287. Let two girls wash and wipe the dishes together, then put a dish of water behind the door with a broom-handle in it. Two men will come in who will be the husbands of the two projectors.
Deer Isle, Me.

288. Run molten lead into hot water ; the shape of the pellets formed shows the occupation of your future sweetheart.
Labrador.

289. Pour molten lead on a hearth ; the shape the metal assumes in cooling foretells the occupation of one's future husband.
General in the United States.

VARIOUS.

290. On accidentally making two lines rhyme, kiss your hand, and you will be so fortunate as to see your lover before nine that night.
Alabama.

291. Put a looking-glass under the pillow, and you will dream of your lover.
Green Harbor, N. F.

292. Tie a true lover's knot (of shavings) and place it under the pillow. You will dream of your lover, even if at that time he is unknown to you. *Newfoundland.*

293. Steal a salt herring from a grocery store, eat it, don't speak after eating, and the first man you dream of will marry you.

294. Make a little ladder of sticks, place it under the head at night, and you'll dream of your future husband. *Patten, Me.*

295. Swallow a chicken's heart whole, and the first man you kiss afterwards will be your future husband. *Winn, Me.*

296. Take three grains of coffee, put one notch on one, two on another, put them in a glass of water under your bed, and name them. The one that sprouts is the one you are going to marry. *Alabama.*

297. Light a match, and the way the flame goes shows where your future husband lives. *Bedford, Mass.*

298. Stand two matches on a hot stove, sulphur end down, and name them for yourself and a marriageable acquaintance of the opposite sex. If both stand or fall together, it is a sign that you will live and die together. If one fall, it is a sign that one will leave the other. *Cape Breton.*

299. Go out in spring and turn up a brick on the ground, and look under it at the clay. The color of the clay denotes the color of the hair of your future husband. *Chestertown, Md.*

300. Cut your finger-nails nine Sundays in succession, and your sweetheart will dine with you. *Alabama.*

301. Throw a ball of yarn into an unoccupied house, and holding the end of the yarn, wind, saying, " I wind and who holds ? " The one who is to be your future wife or husband will be seen in the house. *Ohio.*

302. Take a hair from your head. Have some one else take one from his, cross them, and rub them over each other, and the last thing you say before one breaks will be the first thing said after you are married. *Cambridge, Mass.*

CHAPTER V.

HALLOWEEN AND OTHER FESTIVALS.

Any of the projects quoted in the last chapter are perhaps more likely to be practised on Halloween than at other times. However, as girls do amuse themselves by such fortune-seeking at other times, particularly the first time they sleep in a room, the various projects have been divided into two chapters, according to the way in which the various narrators classed them. That is, when a charm was said to belong to Halloween, it was so classed. When no definite time was set for trying the charm, it was simply put under "projects."

303. A Halloween custom is to fill a tub with water and drop into it as many apples as there are young folks to try the trick. Then each one must kneel before the tub and try to bite the apples without touching them with the hands. The one who bites one first will marry first. *Alabama.*

304. On Halloween hang an apple by the door just the height of the chin. Rub the chin with saliva, stand about six inches from the apple, and hit the chin against the apple. If it sticks to the chin, you will be married, and your true love will stick to you.
St. John, N. B.

305. A girl goes to a field on Halloween at midnight to steal cabbages. The first one whom she meets on her return will be her husband. *Boston, Mass.*

306. On Halloween at midnight a young lady in her night-dress walks backward into the garden and pulls up a cabbage. She will see her future husband over her shoulder.
Eastern Massachusetts.

307. I wind, I wind, my true love to find,
The color of his hair, the clothes he 'll wear,
The day he is married to me.

Throw a ball of yarn into a barn, old house, or cellar, and wind, repeating the above lines, and the true love will appear and wind with you. To be tried at twelve o'clock at night, on Halloween.
Maine.

308. Shortly before midnight a pure white bowl is procured, that has never been touched by any lips save those of a new-born infant. If it is a woman whose fortune is to be tried (and it generally is) the child must be a male. The bowl is filled with water from a spring-well, after which twenty-six pieces of white paper about an inch square, on each of which must be written one letter of the alphabet, are placed in the bowl with the letters turned downward. These must be dropped in as the clock strikes midnight, or all will fail. All being ready, the maiden interested repeats the lines : —

> Kind fortune, tell me where is he
> Who my future lord shall be ;
> From this bowl all that I claim
> Is to know my lover's name.

The bowl is then securely locked away, and must not be disturbed till sunrise the following morning, when she is placed before it blindfolded. She then picks out the same number of letters as there are in her own name. After these are all out the bandage is removed from her eyes, and the paper letters spread out before her. She manages them so as to spell a man's name as best she can with the letters at her disposal. The name thus found will be that of her future husband. *Trinity and Catalina Bays, N. F.*

309. On Halloween a girl is to go through a graveyard, steal a cabbage and place it above the house-door. The one on whom the cabbage falls as the door is opened is to be the girl's husband.
Massachusetts.

310. On Halloween walk backwards from the front door, pick up dust or grass, bring it in, wrap it in paper, put it under your pillow, and dream. *Pennsylvania.*

311. On Halloween put an egg to roast before the fire and leave the doors and windows open. When it begins to sweat a cat will come in and turn it. After the cat will come the man you are to marry, and he will turn it. If you are to die unmarried, the shadow of a coffin will appear. *Chestertown, Md.*

312. On Halloween go upstairs backwards, eating a hard boiled egg without salt, and looking in the glass. You will see your future husband in the glass, looking over your shoulder.
St. John, N. B.

313. On Halloween go down the cellar stairs backward, carrying a mirror into which you look. A face will be seen over your shoulder which will be that of your future husband.
General in the United States.

314. On the last night of October place a mirror and a clock in a room that has not been used for some time, and at a quarter to twelve take a lighted candle and an apple, and finish eating the apple just as the clock strikes twelve, and then look in the mirror and you will see your future husband. *Alabama.*

315. On Halloween put a ring in a dish of mashed potatoes, and the one who gets the ring will be married first. *Boston, Mass.*

316. On Halloween mash potatoes and conceal in the mass a ring, a coin, and a button. Divide it into as many portions as there are persons present. The ring denotes marriage, the coin riches, and the button misfortune. *Massachusetts.*

317. "Silent Supper." On Halloween set a table as if for supper, with as many seats at the table as there are girls, each girl standing behind a chair at the table. The one you are to marry will come in and take the chair in front of you.
Chestertown, Md.

318. On Halloween write names of three men on three pieces of paper, roll them into balls, put these into balls made of Indian meal (wet so as to roll up), put the balls of meal into a basin of water: whichever one rises to the top bears the name of the one you'll marry. *Salem, Mass.*

319. On Halloween, girls place three saucers beside each other, two filled with earth and water, in the other a ring. They are respectively death, cloister or unmarried life, and marriage.
Convent School, Manchester, N. H.

320. On Easter Monday, put on one black garter and one yellow one, and wear them constantly, and you'll have a proposal before the year is out. *Chestertown, Md.*

321. Knit a garter and color it yellow. Don it on Easter Day. Wear it for a year. The wearer will be engaged before the year is out. *Salem, Mass.*

322. On May first look in an unused well, and you'll see the face of your future husband or wife. *New Hampshire.*

323. If you look into a well at exactly twelve o'clock, on the first day of May, through a smoked glass, you will see your future husband. *Alabama.*

324. Hold a mirror over a well on **May first**, and you will see the image of your future husband or wife. 　　　　*Talladega, Ala.*

325. On Midsummer's Day wet a new garment in running water and hang across a chair, wrong side out, to dry. At twelve noon or midnight the one who is to marry you will be seen turning the garment. 　　　　*Labrador.*

326. Place an egg in a tumbler on St. John's Day. The tumbler being half filled with water, an egg is broken into it at early dawn, and it is placed in the window, where it remains untouched till sundown. At that time the broken egg is supposed to have assumed a special shape, in which the ingenious maiden sees dimly outlined the form of her future lord, or some emblem of his calling.

　　　　Newfoundland.

CHAPTER VI.

LOVE AND MARRIAGE.

ENGAGEMENT.

327. If you are a bridesmaid three times you will never stand in the middle. *Baldwinsville, N. Y.*

328. Three times a bridesmaid, never a bride.
New England.

329. Don't let another person put on your engagement ring, taken from your finger, or the engagement will be broken.
Bathurst, N. B.

330. The mother-in-law's test of the incoming daughter-in-law is to place a broom on the floor. If the daughter removes it and places it on one side, she will be a good housewife; if she steps over it, she will be a bad housewife. *Labrador.*

331. A girl will have as many children after marriage as she has "holders" given her before marriage. *Eastern Massachusetts.*

ATTIRE OF THE BRIDE.

332. If you try on your wedding dress before the ceremony, you will not be happy. *Cambridge, Mass.*

333. The bride should wear a borrowed garter, and also a yellow garter. *Boston, Mass.*

334. If a bride wear a yellow garter tied on by a girl friend, the latter will be married inside the year. *Eastern Massachusetts.*

335. The bride should wear

Something old,
Something new,
Something borrowed,
And something blue.
Very common.

336. Wear no black at a wedding ; it foretells ill luck.
Massachusetts.

337. To be married in a brown dress is good luck ; black is bad.
Bathurst, N. B.

338. To be married in anything but white garments indicates bad luck for the bride, white being emblematical of innocence.

They say that white is a heavenly hue.

Another has added,

It may be so, but the sky is blue.
Massachusetts.

339. White is emblematical of holiness and truth. Blue is emblematical of peace and security ; bright green of true learning, as being the uniform clothing of nature.
Maine and Massachusetts.

340. A bride must not look in the glass after her toilet is complete, *i. e.*, she must add a glove or some article after leaving the mirror.
Maine and Massachusetts.

341. It is bad luck for a bride to keep any of the pins that she used when she was married.
Alabama.

342. You will be unhappy if you lose your wedding ring.
General in the United States.

343. If the bride just before leaving the house throws her bouquet over the banisters, the one who catches it is next to be wedded.
Philadelphia, Pa.

344. If a drop of blood gets on a garment in making, it will be one of your wedding garments.

LUCKY DAYS.

345. Marry in Lent,
Live to repent.
New York.

346. The day after a wedding is called the bride's day, the next day the groom's day ; the condition of the weather on these days will indicate whether their lives are to be happy or otherwise.
Salem, Mass., and Queen Anne Co., Md.

347. The wedding day is the bride's day, and the weather foretells her married life. The following is the bridegroom's, and his married life is shown in the same manner. The third day shows how they will live together.
New York.

348. The two days before the wedding are the bride's days. If they are pleasant, she will have good luck, etc.
Waltham, Mass.

349. Marriage days.
Monday — a bad day.
Tuesday — you will have a good husband and will live long.
Wednesday — a grand day ; you will have a good husband, and will live happily, but will have some trouble.
Thursday — a bad day.
Friday — a bad day.
Saturday — no luck at all.
Sunday — no luck at all. *Baltimore, Md. (negro).*

350. Wednesday is the luckiest day on which to be married. Saturday is the unluckiest. Friday is also unlucky.
Bathurst, N. B.

THE MARRIAGE CEREMONY.

351. Happy is the bride that the sun shines on.
Northern Ohio.

352. If it rains on the wedding, the bride will cry all her married life. *Talladega, Ala.*

353. To marry in a storm betokens an unhappy life.
Peabody, Mass.

354. It is unlucky to drop the ring at the marriage ceremony.
New York.

355. A bride must step over the church sill with her right foot.
Orange Co., N. Y.

356. A double wedding is unlucky ; one of the marriages will be unhappy. *Massachusetts.*

357. The pair to be married should stand in line with the cracks in the floor, and not at right angles to them. *Omaha, Neb.*

358. When a couple are married and are driving off, if old shoes are thrown after them for good luck, and one of the shoes lodges on the coach or carriage, it is a sign that one of the party will die before the year is out. *Waltham, Mass.*

359. After the marriage ceremony is performed, the one that walks first from the altar is the one who will die first, either bride or groom. *Alabama.*

360. Old slippers or rice must be thrown after a bride for good luck. *General in the United States.*

361. If the younger sister is married before the elder, the latter will have to dance in a pig's trough. *Western Massachusetts.*

362. Runaway matches will prove unlucky. *New York.*

363. It is a sign of ill luck to take off the wedding ring. *General in the United States.*

COURTING AND WEDDING SIGNS.

364. If your apron string becomes loosened, your true love is thinking of you. *New York.*

365. If your apron drops off, you'll lose your beau. The same is true if you lose your garter. *Stevens Point, Wis.*

366. If you sink a bottle in water, it will weaken your love. *Massachusetts.*

367. Step over the broom, and you will be an old maid.

368. If a girl wet her apron in washing, it is a sign that she will have a drunken husband. *Labrador, Scilly Cove, N. F., and New England.*

369. To hang clothes wrong side out is an antidote for a drunken husband. *Maine.*

370. If a girl finds a cobweb in the door, it is a sign that her beau calls elsewhere. *Northern Ohio.*

371. To find many cobwebs in the kitchen means that there is no courting there. *Boston, Mass.*

372. When the collar slips around and the opening comes to the ear, your lover is thinking of you. *Salem, Mass.*

373. If you button your dress up unevenly, it is a sign that your lover is thinking of you. *Miramichi, N. B.*

374. If you begin to button your dress unevenly, you will be a widow. *Central Maine.*

375. If you are cross when you are young, you will be an old maid.
Alabama.

376. If you fall up stairs, you will have a new beau.
Winn, Me.

377. Tumble up stairs and you 'll not get married within the year. (Hence old maids were formerly said to be careful how they went up stairs.) *New England.*

378. Stumbling either up or down stairs means you 'll be married inside a year. *Cape Breton.*

379. If you sit on a table, you will not be married that year.
New England, New York, and Alabama.

380. Dropping hairpins from your hair means that your beau is thinking of you. *General in the United States.*

381. If a lady dons a gentleman's hat, it is a sign that she wants a kiss.

382. If your lips itch, it is a sign some one will kiss you.
Boston, Mass.

383. If the outside of your nose itches, some one out of town loves you, and if the inside of your nose, then you are loved by some one in town. *Western Massachusetts.*

384. If a gentleman and lady are riding and are tipped out, they will be married. *Nashua, N. H.*

385. Make a rhyme when talking, and you 'll see your true love before Saturday night. *Massachusetts.*

386. Should your shoestring come unloosened,
  'T is a sure sign and a true,
  At that very moment
  Your true love thinks of you.
New York.

387. If your shoe comes untied, your sweetheart is talking about you. *Alabama.*

388. If you want to sneeze and can't, it is a sign some one loves you, and does n't dare to tell it. *Boston, Mass.*

389. If you can't drink a cup of tea, you must be love-sick.
Labrador.

390. Stub your toe
See your beau.
Massachusetts and Maine.

391. If four persons cross hands in shaking hands on taking leave, one will marry before the year is out.
Prince Edward Island, Eastern Massachusetts, and New York.

392. If hands are crossed at the table while passing a dish, a wedding will follow. The top hand belongs to the person who will be married.   *Pennsylvania.*

393. To have two teaspoons in a saucer signifies marriage in a year.

394. If a gentleman stayed to dinner and by accident got two knives, two forks, or two spoons, at his plate, he would be married within a year, and there was no help for it.   *Connecticut.*

395. Knock over your chair on rising from the table, and you won't get married that year.
Peabody, Mass., New York, and Talladega, Ala.

396. If a girl sew a button on the clothing of a marriageable man, she will marry him within the year.   *New England.*

397. If you have a dress with rings for a figure in it, it is a sign you will be married before it is worn out.   *New York.*

398. If you have hearts in a figure in a dress or in a shawl, you will be married before it is worn out.   *New York.*

399. If you have a new dress and there are roses in it, the person who owns the dress will be married before the dress is worn out.
Salem, Mass.

400. Pins in the front of a dress waist are a sign that the wearer will be an old maid.   *New Hampshire.*

401. If, in making a dress, the thread kinks badly, the person for whom it is made will either die or get married before the dress is worn out.   *Alabama.*

402. If you have a dress tried on, and any pin catches in the underclothing, every pin means that it is a year before you will be married ; hence dressmakers are especially careful to pin the dress in such a way that it will slip off easily.   *Boston, Mass.*

403. If you have good success in building a fire, you will have a smart husband; if bad success, a lazy husband.

St. John, N. B., and Ohio.

404. If a lock of hair over the forehead ("widow's lock") be cut before marriage, the girl will be a widow. *Labrador.*

405. Get a lady friend to knit you a yellow garter. She must ask a gentleman unknown to you to knit ten rows. You will meet and marry the gentleman within a year.

406. The exchange of one yellow garter means a proposal in six months. *Washington, D. C.*

407. If a girl wears a yellow garter (which has been given to her) every day for a year, or every day and night for six months, at the end of that time she will be married. *Montreal, P. Q.*

408. If you burn a lover's letter, he will never marry you.

Central Maine.

409. If, at a dinner, a single person is inadvertently placed between two married people (husband or wife), it means marriage for him or her within a year.

410. If you pass between two men on the street, you'll marry both of them sometime. *Champaign, Ill.*

411. If you drop a knitting-needle, you won't be married during the present year.

412. If you break many needles in a garment, it will be worn at a wedding.

413. If you draw blood from a prick of the needle while making a garment, it is a sign you will be kissed the first time you wear it.

Boston, Mass.

414. Should needles break while sewing on a new garment, it is a sign that the owner will be married before it is worn out.

New York.

415. When a young man goes to see a girl for the first time, and the signs of the zodiac are in the heart, they will one day marry.

Harmony, Me.

416. If you step on a cigar stub, you will marry the first man you meet. *Salem, Mass.*

417. Two spoons in a cup is the sign of a wedding.

Bathurst, N. B., and Wisconsin.

418. If you get two spoons in your cup or saucer, you 'll marry a second husband or wife.

419. If a couple out walking together stumble, it is a sign that they will be married.　　　*Labrador.*

420. Sit on the table,
　　Married before you 're able.

Mattawamkeag, Me.

421. If a girl gets the last piece of bread on a plate at the table, she will have a handsome husband.　　*Massachusetts.*

422. If all of three dishes at the table are eaten, all of the unmarried people at the table will be married within the year.

Northern Massachusetts.

423. "If the tea-kettle boils, you will boil your beaux away," is an old saying.　　　*Salem, Mass.*

424. If you have a cup of tea handed to you, and there are little bits floating on top, they represent the number of husbands you will have — one, two, or three.

425. A girl that takes her thimble to the table will be an old maid.　　　*Northern Ohio.*

426. Three in a row,
　　Meet your beau.
　　The one in the middle will have him.

Massachusetts.

427. Three lamps in a row, the one who sets down the third will be soon married.　　　*Massachusetts.*

428. Three lamps in a row foretell a wedding in the family.

New York.

429. To look into a tumbler when you are drinking is a sign that you will be an old maid.　If you look over the side, you are a flirt.

Massachusetts.

430. To wash the hands under a pump denotes that you will be a widow.　　　*Chestertown, Md.*

CHAPTER VII.

WISHES.

431. IF you take a baby in your arms for the first time, and at the same time wish, you will get your wish before the year is out.

Quebec.

432. Take your Bible and wish. If it opens at "and it came to pass," you will get your wish.

433. Wish upon a candle on blowing it out. If it glows long, you will get your wish. If it smokes, it signifies a death. *Ohio.*

434. If a speck of carbon comes on the wick when burning, and you wish for something, wet your finger and touch the speck. If it sticks to your finger, you will get the wish, and *vice versa.*

Plymouth, O.

435. Swallow a chicken's heart whole and make a wish. It will come true. *Pennsylvania and Ohio.*

436. Throw an egg out of the second story window and wish. If it does not break, you will get your wish. *Deer Isle, Me.*

437. Throw an eyelash over your shoulder. If it falls from your finger in doing this, your wish will come true. If it remains on the finger, your wish will not come to pass. *New York.*

438. Find a stray eyelash ; place it on the back of the hand with a wish ; blow it off. If it blows off at the first trial, the wish will come true. *St. John, N. B., and Pennsylvania.*

439. Put a loose eyelash on the back of your hand. It signifies a letter. Wish from whom the letter may come, carry it three times around your head, then throw it over your shoulder, and you will get your wish. *New England.*

440. Put an eyewinker down inside your clothes, wish, and you'll get your wish. *Maine.*

441. Put an eyewinker on the back of the hand, knock that hand with the other so as to throw the eyewinker over the shoulder, and at the same time wish. If the eyewinker is not seen again, the wish will come true. *Stoneham, Mass.*

442. If you wish on the first thing you eat in the season, the wish will come true.

443. Wish with two paper slips or grass blades, the ends only being shown. The longer wins.

444. Wish on a load of hay, and you 'll be sure to get it. *Winn, Me.*

445. Wish when you see a hay-cart, don't look at it again, and you 'll get the wish. *New Jersey.*

446. See a white horse; don't look at his tail, but wish.

447. Wish on a " calico " horse.

448. You may wish on a row of empty barrels, or on a piebald horse, but you must not look on the object a second time.

449. Wish on a load of empty barrels, and you will get your wish. *Peabody, Mass.*

450. Write the names of one hundred people who (by request) have bowed to you, bury the paper in a secret spot, and at the same time wish. If no one sees you, you will get your wish.

451. Wish while holding a lighted match until it is extinct, and you 'll get the wish.

452. If by chance two use the same words, lock the little fingers, and wish before speaking, saying " Shakespeare " at the end. *Eastern Massachusetts.*

453. Let two persons break the wishing-bone of a fowl; the one who gets the longest piece will get his wish. *New Jersey and Ohio.*

454. If you say two sentences that rhyme, make a wish, then if you make a rhyme unintentionally and wish before you speak again, your wish will come to pass. *Baldwinsville, N. Y.*

455. When you first see a sleigh in the fall of the year, make a wish, and you will get it. *Winn, Me.*

456. Wish at the first snowflake of the season, and you will get your wish. *Westport, Mass.*

457. Put a ring on the finger of another person, saying, " I wish it on until such a time," and if it is not removed before the expiration of the period named, the wish will come to pass.
Connecticut and Ohio.

458. When you see a falling star, wish. *New Jersey.*

459. To wish on a star, when you see the first star come out, say :

> Star light, star bright,
>> First star I see to-night,
> I wish I may, I wish I might
>> Have the wish I wish to-night.

Wish what you please and it will come true, but the wish must not be mentioned to any one. *Eastern Massachusetts.*

460. Count nine evening stars in succession, and you will have your wish. *Massachusetts.*

461. Capture a floating thistledown, breathe on it, make a wish to see or hear from an absent friend, blow in his or her supposed direction, and it will carry your message. *Ohio.*

462. Make a wish while throwing a leaf into running water. If it lands right side up, you will have your wish or good luck.
Lebanon, N. H.

CHAPTER VIII.

DREAMS.

ANIMALS.

463. To dream of cod or caplin is a sign of rain

Newfoundland.

464. To dream of a good catch of fish is a sign of rain.

Heart's Content, N. F.

465. To dream of catching fish is good luck.

Prince Edward Island.

466. If you dream you catch fish, it is a sign you will make a good bargain, according to the size of the fish.

467. To dream of catching a fish means money.	*Cape Breton.*

468. To dream of flies means sickness.	*Massachusetts.*

469. To dream of flies is good luck.	*Peabody, Mass.*

470. To dream of lice is a sign of death.	*New Harbor, N. F.*

471. To dream of lice is a sign of enemies.	*Topsail, N. F.*

472. To dream of lice is a sign of " coming wealth."

Alabama.

473. To dream of lice means sickness in the family.	*Ohio.*

474. To dream of snakes means enemies.

*Cape Breton.	General in the United States.*

In some localities it is said if you kill the snake in your dream you will conquer your enemies.

475. To dream of porpoises is bad luck.	*Labrador.*

476. It is lucky to dream of pigs.	*Bruynswick, N. Y.*

477. Dreaming of (or seeing) rats (numerous) is a sign of death.

Heart's Content, N. F.

478. To dream of a rat is the sign of an enemy.   *Boston, Mass.*

479. To dream of rats is a sign of thieves.
Central Maine and Chestertown, Md.

480. It is a sign of bad news to dream about a white horse.
Quebec.

481. To dream of a white horse three nights in succession is a sign of the death of an elderly person.   *Central New York.*

482. To dream of a white horse is a sign some one of the family will die within a year.   *Maine.*

483. To dream of three white colts is a sign of a young person dying.   *Central New York.*

484. If you dream of a black horse, it is a sure sign of death.
Peabody, Mass.

485. To dream of a black horse is a sign of a wedding ; of a white horse is a sign of a letter.   *Cape Breton.*

486. To dream of a horse is a sign of a letter.
Miramichi, N. B.

487. To dream of horses is a sign of wind.   *Topsail, N. F.*

488. Dreaming of cows is a sign of a hostile, angry woman.
Bay Roberts, N. F.

489. To dream of dogs and horses is a sign of good luck.
St. John, N. B.

490. To dream of catching a bird is a sign of a letter.
Cape Breton.

491. If you dream of a bird in a cage you will have trouble with your beau.   *New England.*

492. To dream of cats means enemies.   *Cape Breton.*

493. To dream of a cat means an enemy.   If in the dream you conquer the cat, you will conquer the enemy.   *Miramichi, N. B.*

COLORS.

494. To dream of white things is lucky (or sign of death ?).
Newfoundland.

495. Dreaming of white things is a sign of snow in summer.
Labrador and Newfoundland.

496. Dreaming of working on white cloth is a sign of death.
Newfoundland.

497. To dream of white or red is unlucky.   To dream of black is lucky.

DEAD PERSONS.

498. To dream of a dead father is lucky.   *Labrador.*

499. To dream of a dead mother is unlucky; it brings sorrow.
Labrador.

500. To dream of the dead is a sign of hearing from the living.
Topsail and New Harbor, N. F.

501. To dream of the dead is a sign of rain.
New Harbor, N. F.

502. To dream of seeing a deceased friend means rain within a few days.   *Talladega, Ala.*

503. To dream of a dead person means a letter next day.
Northern Maine.

504. If you dream of the dead, you'll hear from the living.
Prince Edward Island ; General in the United States.

EARTH.

505. To dream of walking in a garden is a sign of a graveyard.

506. To dream of ploughed ground indicates that a grave will be dug for some member of the family before the year ends.
Western New York.

507. To dream of seeing fresh earth bodes misfortune.
Northern Ohio.

508. To dream of digging ground, or white potatoes, is a sign of death.   *Harbor Grace, N. F.*

509. To dream of seeing the ground unseasonably ploughed means death.   *Nova Scotia.*

EGGS.

510. To dream of eggs means you will get a beating.
Prince Edward Island.

511. Dreaming of eggs is a sign of anger ; if broken, all over.
New Harbor, N. F.

512. To dream of whole eggs is a sign of a "fuss ;" of broken eggs is not.   *Chestertown, Md.*

513. To dream of a nest full of eggs and a bird sitting on them means you will receive something new. *Cape Breton.*

FIRE AND SMOKE.

514. It is bad luck to dream of fire. *St. John, N. B.*

515. To dream of fire portends sickness.
Eastern Massachusetts.

516. If you dream of fire, it is a sign of trouble in the family.
Alabama.

517. If you dream of fire, you 'll have a row. *Massachusetts.*

518. To dream of fire is a sign of anger.
Newfoundland and Labrador.

519. To dream of fire means hasty news. To dream of smoke means trouble. *Miramichi, N. B.*

520. Dream of flame out of season,
You will be angry without a reason.

521. If you dream about a large blaze of fire, you will get some money unexpectedly. *Alabama.*

522. Dreaming of smoke indicates trouble. *Alabama.*

523. To dream of smoke means death. *Wisconsin.*

HUMAN BEINGS.

524. To dream of a baby is a sign of death.

525. To dream of babies is unlucky or is a sign of trouble.
General in the United States.

526. To dream of carrying a child is unlucky.

527. It is bad luck or death to dream of naked clinging (climbing ?) children. *Labrador and Newfoundland.*

528. It is ill luck to dream of a priest. *Central Maine.*

529. If you dream of a negro, you will surely quarrel.

530. If you dream of being kissed by or being very intimate with a woman friend, it means a disagreement.

531. If you dream of a person of the opposite sex three nights in succession, you are sure to marry him.   *Alabama.*

532. If you dream of a gentleman, you will never marry him.
     Bedford, Mass.

533. If you dream of a person as going two ways at once, it is a sign the person dreamed of will die before the year is out.
     Boston, Mass.

534. To dream of a naked man is a sign of the death of a woman, and *vice versa.*   *Baltimore, Md. (negro).* ·

535. To dream of a drunken husband or man is unlucky.
     Labrador.

536. To dream of men is lucky.   *Newfoundland.*

537. To dream of women is unlucky.   *Bay Roberts, N. F.*

METEOROLOGICAL PHENOMENA.

538. To dream of walking through snow means sickness.
     St. John, N. B.

539. To dream of a snowstorm is a sign of the speedy death of a relative.   *South Framingham, Mass.*

540. To dream of snow in spring (May) is a sign of a good catch of fish.   *Trinity Bay, N. F.*

541. If a fisherman dreams of its raining, it is a sign of a good catch of fish.   *Green Harbor, N. F.*

542. Anything dreamed "on the east wind," *i. e.,* when the east wind is blowing, will come true.   *Chestertown, Md. (negro).*

MONEY AND METALS.

543. To dream of silver money is a sign of sickness.

544. To dream of small change (money) is bad luck.
     Newfoundland.

545. To dream of gold or silver is good luck ; of paper is bad.
     Boston, Mass.

546. If you dream of gold, it is a sign of an increase of property.
     Alabama.

TEETH.

547. To dream of teeth is unlucky.   *Eastern Massachusetts.*

548. It is death or bad luck to dream of teeth falling out.
Newfoundland and Northern Ohio.

549. To dream of losing a tooth means a death.
Nova Scotia and Cape Breton.

550. To dream of pulling out your teeth means sickness.
Eastern Massachusetts.

551. To dream of losing a tooth means losing a friend.
Virginia.

552. If you dream of having a front tooth drop out, you will lose a near relative within a year.   If a back tooth, a distant relative.

WATER.

553. To dream of smooth water means good luck ; of rough water means ill luck.   *St. John, N. B.*

554. Dreaming of running water means approaching death to the dreamer or some near relative.

555. To dream of clear, sparkling water means good luck.
Miramichi, N. B.

556. To dream of milky or roily water means death or disaster.
Miramichi, N. B.

557. To dream of seeing muddy water signifies that you will have trouble.   *Alabama.*

558. To dream of clear water means prosperity ; of muddy water means trouble.   *Boston, Mass.*

559. To dream of washing is a sign of a move.
Cape Breton and Wisconsin.

WEDDINGS AND FUNERALS.

560. To dream of marriage is a sign of a funeral.
Topsail and Carbonear, Trinity Bay, N. F.

561. If you dream of a marriage, it is the sign of a death ; and if you dream of a death, it is the sign of a marriage.   *Alabama.*

562. If you dream of a marriage, you will hear of a death next day.
Talladega, Ala.

563. If you dream of a wedding, you will hear of the death of a friend in that month. *Pennsylvania.*

564. To dream of a wedding means death.

Mifflintown, Pa.

565. Dream on a piece of wedding cake. Write names on slips of paper and pull them out. The one you pull twice is the one you will marry. *Massachusetts.*

566. Sleep on a piece of wedding cake, and the one you dream about will be your future partner in life. *New Brunswick.*

567. Sleep on a piece of wedding cake, and if you have the same dream three nights in succession, your dream will come to pass.

New York.

568. To dream of a funeral means a wedding.

MISCELLANEOUS.

569. To dream of raw meat is a sign of ill luck.

570. To dream of eating meat is a sign of sickness.

Boston.

571. To see while asleep fresh meats of any kind is a warning of death. *Alabama.*

572. To dream of blood is a sign of sickness. *Alabama.*

573. To dream of blood is a sign that some one will "scandalize" you. *Baltimore, Md. (negro).*

574. To dream of onions is good.

575. To dream of flowers is a sign of sickness. *Alabama.*

576. To dream of

Fruit out of season,
Trouble without reason.

Northern Ohio.

577. To dream of cherries is evil.

578. To dream of an anchor means good luck.

St. John, N. B.

579. To dream on land of a vessel (with sails set?) is a sign of a funeral. *Labrador and Trinity Bay, N. F.*

580. To dream of small beads or sewing silk is lucky.

Labrador.

581. What you dream the first night you are in a strange house will come true. *General in the United States.*

582. If you dream the first night you are in a strange bed, your dream will come true. If the dream was of a sweetheart, you will be married. *Trinity Bay and Bay Roberts, N. F.*

583. To dream of losing the sole of your shoe indicates the death of a near friend. *Cape Breton.*

584. To dream of seeing any one wear worn-out shoes means the death of a near relative. *Cape Breton.*

585. To dream of a hole worn in a boot is a sign of being sick.

Newfoundland.

586. To dream of bad boots is unlucky. *Newfoundland.*

587. Saturday night 's dream, Sunday morning told,
Will come to pass before it 's a week old.

Maine and Massachusetts.

588. Saturday night dreamt,
Sunday morning told,
Sure to come true
Before a month old.

Eastern Massachusetts.

589. Relate the dream before breakfast, and it will come true.
General in the United States.

590. If you dream the same thing three times, it will come true.

591. Dreaming of handling new-made boards is a sign of a coffin. (A carpenter's notion.) *Heart's Content, N. F.*

592. If you dream of seeing a boat drawn or sailing on land, it is a sign of death. *Cape Breton.*

593. If you dream that you see an empty coffin, you will see it filled within a year.

594. To dream of dough in a bread pan is the sign of a coffin.
New Brunswick.

595. To dream of dough in a black pan is a sign of a corpse.
Miramichi, N. B.

596. To dream of bread is good luck. *Boston, Mass.*

597. To dream of going in a carriage means you 'll travel with a friend. *Cape Breton.*

598. Pick up a stone in a strange place and put it under the pillow for three nights. If you dream, it will come true.
Newfoundland.

599. To dream of being in a new house is a sign of death.
Harbor Grace, N. F.

600. Place the heel of one shoe against the instep of the other three nights in a row, and you will dream of your future husband.
Franklin, Mass.

601. To dream that your sweetheart has the ague means that he loves you.

602. To dream you are a fool is good luck and increase of wealth.

603. Dreaming of persons being sick is a sign of being well.
Newfoundland and New Hampshire.

604. To dream of a death is a sign of life.

605. To dream of the devil is a sign of good luck.
Trinity Bay, N. F.

606. To dream you cry means you will laugh.
Boston, Mass.

607. Dreams go by contraries. *General in the United States.*

CHAPTER IX.

LUCK.

CARDS.

608. At cards, if your luck is poor, walk round your chair three times, lift it, sit down, and your luck is assured.
General in the United States.

609. At cards, it is bad luck to play against the grain of the table.
General in the United States.

610. At cards, it is unlucky to turn up your hand before the dealer is through. *Alabama.*

611. At cards, it is common to blow on the deal, without looking at it, for good luck. *Providence, R. I., and Salem, Mass.*

DAYS.

612. It is unlucky to travel on Friday.
New York and Pennsylvania.

613. Never begin a piece of work on Friday ; it is bad luck.
General in the United States.

614. Seafaring men will not sail on Friday.
Somewhat general in the United States.

615. If you begin a piece of work on Friday, it will be a very short or a very long job. *St. John, N. B.*

616. It is bad luck to cut your finger-nails on Friday.
Pigeon Cove, Mass.

617. As with the superstitious generally, Friday is a very unlucky day. Housekeepers will prefer paying a quarter's rent extra to going into a house on that day. It is, of course, most unlucky to be married on it. Wednesday is the day considered most favorable for the purpose. *Newfoundland.*

618. If you cut your nails on Sunday, you 'll do something you 're ashamed of before the week is out. *Maine.*

619. If business is transacted on Sunday, you will lose by it on the coming week. *New York.*

620. Pancake Day is Shrove Tuesday. If you do not eat pancakes on that day, you will have no luck throughout the year. The hens won't lay, etc. *Chestertown, Md.*

621. When the two figures that tell one's age are alike, as 22, 33, etc., some great change in life is to be expected. *Nashua, N. H.*

DRESSING.

622. If you put on any garment wrong side out, as, for example, a pair of stockings, never change it, as to do so brings ill luck. This direction is intuitively followed by many people who are entirely free from conscious superstition. *General in the United States.*

623. If you put a garment on wrong side out, you must n't speak of it, or you will have bad luck. *Maine.*

624. If you put a garment on wrong side out, or a hat on wrong end before, spit on it before turning, to prevent bad luck. *Maine and Ohio.*

625. If a garment is put on wrong side out, it is lucky, but unlucky to turn it. *Prince Edward Island and Massachusetts.*

626. To clothe the left foot before the right one is a sign of misfortune. *Ohio.*

627. If you button up your dress wrong, *i. e.*, do not begin with the button and button-hole opposite each other, it means bad luck, or good luck if worn uneven until after sunset. *Cape Breton.*

628. The putting of the left shoe on the right foot, lacing it wrong, or losing a button, are all bad signs. *Alabama.*

629. Walking across the room with one shoe off is a sign of ill luck. *Alabama.*

630. When putting on your shoes and stockings, if you complete dressing one foot before beginning to dress the other, it is a sign you will be disappointed. *Northern Ohio.*

HORSESHOES.

631. It is good luck to find a horseshoe.
General in the United States and Canada.

632. The luck is especially good if the loop end is towards you, that is, if you meet it. *Miramichi, N. B.*

633. If you find horseshoes and pick them up, you will have a horse.

634. The more nails in the horseshoe, the more luck.
Western Pennsylvania.

635. To find a horseshoe nail is good luck, especially if the head is towards you. *Miramichi, N. B.*

636. If horseshoes are put up over a house for luck, the points should not be placed downwards, or the luck will slip through.

PINS.

637. See a pin and pick it up,
All the day you 'll have good luck;
See a pin and pass it by (or "let it lie"),
All the day your luck will fly.
Eastern Massachusetts.

638. See a pin and pick it up,
All the day you 'll have good luck;
See a pin and let it lie,
Come to sorrow by and by.
New York.

639. See a pin and pick it up for luck. If the head is towards you, the luck is slow in coming; if the point is towards you, the luck is quick and sharp. *Boston, Mass.*

640. If you see a pin crosswise, that is, across your path, it means a ride if you pick it up. *Boston, Mass.*

641. "I have known a young lady form a habit of stooping in consequence of keeping the eyes fixed on the ground, in the streets of New York city, in order not to miss the good fortune that might come of picking up a pin. The pin must be thrust into a tree or post, in order to keep the luck as long as it remains fast."
New York, N. Y.

642. Find a pin and let it lie,
You 'll want a pin before you die.
Alabama.

643. See a pin and let it lie,
You 'll want that pin before you die.
Peabody, Mass.

SALT.

644. It is unlucky to pass salt across the table.

645. Spilling salt is unlucky ; throw some over your left shoulder, or burn a pinch to avert ill luck.   *Northern Ohio.*

646. It is bad luck to spill salt unless it is burned.
Virginia.

647. If you spill salt, throw some over your left shoulder, and then crawl under one side of the table and come out on the other, to prevent bad luck.   *Bucks Co., Pa.*

648. Spilling salt at table is ill luck to the one towards whom it is spilled.   *Iowa.*

649. If you spill salt, you will have a whipping.
New England and Canada.

SWEEPING.

650. If the broom is moved with the rest of the household furniture, you will not be successful.   The broom should be burned while standing in the corner, being watched meanwhile, to prevent the house from taking fire.

651. Never sweep the floor after sunset ; it is bad luck.
Alabama.

652. Carrying ashes out of the house after sunset is bad luck.
Virginia.

653. It is ill luck to sweep dirt out of doors after sunset.
Virginia.

654. Dirt must not be swept out of doors after dark, or it will bring disaster to the master of the house.   This belief is common among negroes and superstitious whites.   *Chestertown, Md.*

655. Sailors are unwilling that their friends should sweep after dark, because in that case their wages will be swept away by sickness or otherwise.   *Westport, Mass.*

TURNING BACK.

656. It is unlucky to turn back for anything after you have set out to go anywhere. *Prince Edward Island.*

657. Returning to the house for something and starting again without sitting down is bad luck. *Virginia.*

658. It will prove unlucky if you return for a forgotten article after you have left the house ; but if you seat yourself before leaving the house again, the misfortune will be averted. *New York.*

659. To avert ill luck or disappointment that will come if a person comes back to a house for something forgotten, he must sit down a minute. *General in New England.*

660. To go back into the house for something after starting on a journey is unpropitious. To have it brought out is all right.
Iowa.

661. If you have to go back to the house after something forgotten, you must not sit down, but stand a moment or two, or else it is bad luck. *Cape Breton.*

662. If you start anywhere and go back, it is bad luck unless you make a cross-mark and spit in it. *Alabama and Kentucky.*

MISCELLANEOUS.

663. If two persons shake hands across the gate, they are bringing on themselves ill luck. *Alabama.*

664. It is unlucky to pass under a ladder. *Canada.*

665. Go under a ladder and you will be hanged.

666. Walking under a ladder is considered very unlucky. In the outposts girls will climb the rockiest cliffs to avoid such a contingency. On one occasion in St. John's, where a ladder extended across the sidewalk, of one hundred and twenty-seven girls who came along, only six ventured under it, the rest going along the gutter in mud ankle deep. *Newfoundland.*

667. If, in passing, one parts two people, it is a sign of disappointment to the parter.

668. When two or three people go between different posts, in the entrance of gardens, cemeteries, etc., it is a sign they will be separated or disappointed.   *General in the United States.*

669. Sing on the street,
Disappointment you 'll meet.

670. To count the steps of stairs, as you lie on your back, indicates the number of your troubles.

671. To fall upstairs means good luck; downstairs, ill luck.
                                        Massachusetts.

672. To stumble downstairs, or on going out in the morning, means bad luck.   *Peabody, Mass.*

673. Opals are unlucky.   *General in the United States.*

674. The opal is unlucky, unless set with diamonds.
                                        New York.

675. Don't let the tea-kettle boil so as to make a bubbling or thumping noise, as some say it is unlucky.
                                        Eastern Massachusetts.

676. A tea-kettle boiling so as to make a bubbling sound is said to boil away luck, and should be removed from the flame.
                                        Eastern Massachusetts.

677. Never let your dish-water come to a boil, as every bubble means bad luck to the family.   *Eastern Massachusetts.*

678. Sewing in the twilight is an ill omen.   *Chatham, N. H.*

679. To look over another person's shoulder into a looking-glass means disappointment.   *Deer Isle, Me.*

680. When going fishing, fishermen wear white mittens for luck.
                                        Portsmouth, N. H.

681. It is unlucky to lose a glove.   *Bathurst, N. B.*

682. It is bad luck to have any one step across the fishing-pole; you will catch no fish.   *Talladega, Ala.*

683. Crawl under a fence, and you will have bad luck.
                                        Western Masssachusetts.

684. To step over the feet of any one who is sitting is ill luck.

685. Getting out of bed with the left foot first, or taking anything with the left hand when the right is disengaged, is a sign of bad luck. *Alabama.*

686. In getting out of bed in the morning, the right foot is always to be placed first. *Ohio.*

687. To get out of bed left foot first makes one cross. "He got out of bed left foot first," is a universal saying.

688. In going in at the house door, always put the right foot foremost. This practice is observed by many intelligent people.

689. To sing at the table is a sign you will be disappointed.

690. It is an ill omen to leave the table while eating, to light the lamp. *Western Massachusetts.*

691. To lay the knife and fork crosswise is ill luck.
Peabody, Mass.

692. When you drop a knife or fork, and it sticks up in the floor, you will have good luck.

693. It is lucky to find a rusty knife or other steel instrument.
Maine.

694. If a knife be spun round, care should be taken to spin it back again, otherwise it insures bad luck.

695. Often verses of Proverbs xxxi. are assigned to girls and boys respectively according to the day of the month of the birth.
Labrador and Brookline, Mass.

696. It brings bad luck to the bearer of a ring to have it taken from her finger by another person. *Massachusetts.*

697. Measuring one's waist, as for a dress, will bring ill luck.

698. To turn a loaf of bread upside down is ill luck.
Northern Ohio.

699. To find a four-leaved clover is lucky; but five-leaved, unlucky. *General in the United States.*

700. When a vessel is launched, break a bottle of wine over her for luck. The bottle is to be broken by a lady.
General in the United States.

701. Never carry clean wet clothes from one house to another, as it will bring ill luck.   *Chestertown, Md.*

702. Do not go into your new house by the back door; if you do you take disaster with you.

703. Never build on a spot where a house has been burned. The second house is likely to go in the same manner.
                                        Maine and Massachusetts.

704. Light coming in at the window is a bad sign.
                                        Peabody, Mass.

705. The opening of an umbrella in the house is a sign of bad luck.   *General in the United States.*

706. If you drop your umbrella, you will have ill luck if you pick it up yourself; but the ill luck may be averted by having some one else pick it up.   *Prince Edward Island.*

707. To carry a hoe through the house is ill luck.   *Alabama.*

708. To light three lights with one match is good luck for a week.
                                        Peabody, Mass.

709. The falling of a chandelier foretells a disaster in the family.
                                        New York.

710. Breaking a looking-glass shows that you 'll have seven years of ill luck.   *General in the United States.*

711. If a chair be turned about on one of its forelegs, there will be bad luck in the house all that year.   *Talladega, Ala.*

712. A mare-browed man, that is, one whose eyebrows meet, is unlucky and can cast spells.   *Newfoundland.*

713. It is unlucky, when going deer-hunting, to meet a red-haired man.   *Newfoundland.*

CHAPTER X.

MONEY.

714. A GROUP of bubbles on a cup of coffee signifies money.
United States.

715.—A mass of bubbles floating on a cup of coffee signifies that money is coming to one. If he can take up the bubbles on his spoon, it indicates that he will get the money, but if they escape he will not. *Prince Edward Island.*

716. If a group of bubbles are floating on the tea or coffee cup, take them up in a spoon, and swallow them unbroken, saying, " Save my money." *Plymouth and Salem, Mass., and New Brunswick.*

717. If when you stir your coffee at breakfast you will try to catch the bubbles on top, you can have as many dollars as you can catch whole ones. *Alabama.*

718. To find money and keep it insures good luck through the year. *Talladega, Ala.*

719. Put the first piece of money you get in the morning into your stocking, and you will have more to add to it before night.
Alabama.

720. If you find a piece of money the first day of the year, you will have good luck all the rest of the year. *Alabama.*

721. If paper money is folded lengthwise first, it will insure the possession of money. If folded the short fold first, money will not remain in the pocket. *Alabama.*

(722. To make a sale in the first place where an agent calls is good luck.)For example, a magnifying-glass worth three dollars was sold for seventy-five cents, in order to stop a run of bad luck by making a sale. *Massachusetts.*

723. If your initials spell a word, it means that you will be rich.
Massachusetts and Ohio.

724. If the right hand itches, it is a sign you will receive money; if the left, you will spend money, because *R* stands for receive, and *L* for let go. *New York.*

725. If the left hand itches and you rub it on wood, you 'll receive money before the end of the week.

Rub it on wood
To make it good.

Very common in New Brunswick and New England.

726. Itching in the palm of the hand means that it will soon receive money. Clap the closed hand into the pocket. *Mt. Desert, Me.*

727. If you place your money according to value, *i. e.*, lay it in order, you will be rich. *Bedford, Mass.*

728. An old superstition pertaining to clothing is, that before putting on new clothes a sum of money must be placed in the right-hand pocket, which will insure its always being full. If by mistake, however, it be put in the left hand pocket, the wearer will never have a penny so long as the clothes last.

729. There 's a "bag of money," or a " pot of gold," at the end of the rainbow. *General among children.*

730. If you sew in the twilight, you will never be rich. *Miramichi, N. B.*

731. If you mend or sew on a garment while wearing it, you will always be poor. *Bathurst, N. B.*

732. Always shut the doors, or you will never own a house. *Salem, Mass.*

733. Sparks in the soot on the back wall above a coal fire bring wealth. *Rhode Island.*

734. Say "Money" three times at sight of a meteor, and you 'll get it, or wish and you 'll get it.

735. When you see a shooting star, say "money." As many times as you are able to repeat the word during the fall of the star, so many dollars you will have in your pocket. *Connecticut.*

CHAPTER XI.

VISITORS.

736. HAVING a piece of bread and taking another is a sign some one is coming hungry. *Maine, New York, and Pennsylvania.*

737. If you drop a slice of bread with the buttered side up, it is a sign of a visitor. *Bathurst, N. B.*

738. If a broom falls across the threshold, it means a visitor is coming. *Massachusetts.*

739. Three chairs in a row is a sign of a caller. *Bedford, Mass.*

740. Two chairs chancing to be placed back to back denote that a visitor is coming. *Danvers, Mass.*

741. One chair in front of another means a stranger. *Peabody, Mass.*

742. If you go around the chimney without sitting down, you will bring company to that house. *Guilford, Conn.*

743. Company on Sunday means company all the week. *New England.*

744. If you have company on Monday, you will have company every day in the week. *General in the United States.*

745. If you drop the dish-cloth, it is a sign you will have company. *General in the United States.*

746. If you almost drop a dish-cloth and catch it before it falls, it is a sign of a visitor. *Bathurst, N. B.*

747. If you drop a dish-rag, some one is coming hungry. *Alabama.*

748. If the dish-cloth on falling to the floor spreads out, the visitor will be a lady ; if it falls in a heap, it will be a gentleman. *Cape Breton and Central Maine.*

749. If you drop the tea-towel, it is a sign of company.

Pennsylvania.

750. If you go in at one door and out at another, it is a sign of company.   *New York and Ohio.*

751. Going out through one door of the house and in through another means a visit from agreeable company.

752. If you go in at one door and out of another of the house of a friend, a stranger will enter the house soon.

Central New Hampshire.

753. If you go in at the back (or front) door of a house, and out at the front (or back) without sitting down, you will bring company.

Guilford, Conn.

754. If you forget anything on your departure from a visit, you will go there again.   *Eastern Massachusetts.*

755. If the fork is dropped at the table, a man will call.

Pennsylvania.

756. If you drop a fork, and it sticks in the floor and remains in a standing position, it is a sign that a gentleman will call; but if a knife, a lady will call.   *General in the United States.*

757. Should you drop a knife or scissors so that they stick into the floor and stand up, it is a sign of company.   *New York.*

758. The dropping of any sharp-pointed instrument which sticks up in the floor, such as a knife, a pair of scissors, etc., foretells company coming from the direction in which the article leans.

Massachusetts.

759. If the scissors drops there will be visitors; if the small blade sticks in the floor it will be children; if the large, adults.

Nashua, N. H.

760. A needle dropping on the floor and sticking up means visitors.   *St. John, N. B.*

761. If a knife be dropped at table, a woman will call.

Pennsylvania.

762. If you drop a knife at table, a lady will come during the evening; if a fork, a gentleman is coming.   *Talladega, Ala.*

763. If you drop a knife, your visitor will be a woman; if a fork, it will be a man; if a spoon, it will be a fool.   *Pennsylvania.*

764. If you drop a knife, it is a sign a lady is coming to see you. If a fork, the visitor will be a man ; if a spoon, your cousin.

New York.

765. Two knives beside a plate mean a lady stranger; two forks, a man. *Peabody, Mass.*

766. To put two spoons in your teacup is a sign of a stranger.

Maine and Massachusetts.

767. Two forks or spoons crossed on a plate signify that a stranger is coming.

768. If you wash the sugar-bowl, you will have company.

Eastern Massachusetts.

769. To have too many plates on the table means guests.

770. If an extra plate be accidentally placed upon the table, some visitor will come hungry. *Northern Ohio.*

771. If you are offered an article of food at the table, which you already have on your plate, but forgetting that you have it, take some more, it is a sign that a stranger is coming to your house before you eat another meal. *Quebec.*

772. If stems of tea-grounds are found in the cup, it denotes that visitors are coming. If you wish them to come, bite the heads off and throw them under the table. *Deerfield, Mass.*

773. If the stems of tea-grounds come on top of the cup, visitors are coming. Bite one, and if it is hard, it will be a man ; if soft, a woman. *New Hampshire.*

774. If successful in the attempt to take stems from your tea, a friend is going to visit you. *Alabama.*

775. If a tea-stem is on top of the cup, put it in your shoe, and you will have company. *Massachusetts.*

776. If a tea-stem floats in the tea, it is a sign you will have a visitor. If it is hard, it is a man ; if it is soft, it is a woman. If it is long, the visitor will be tall ; if short, the visitor will be short.

New York.

777. To learn about visitors from tea-grounds : Lift the leaf out and press it against the left hand, naming the days of the week.

Upon whichever day the leaf chances to cling and rest, company may be expected. To complete the spell, put the leaf down your neck and wish.   *Plymouth, Mass.*

778. If your eye quivers, a stranger is coming.   *Labrador.*

779. If a stray hair blows persistently across the eyes, it's the sign that a stranger is coming.   *Massachusetts.*

780. The shin-bone itching means guests.

781. The nose itching signifies visitors.
                    General in the United States.

782. The nose itching foretells company. If on the right side, it means a man ; if on the left, a woman.   *Central New York.*

783. If your nose itches, you will see an old friend whom you have not seen for some time.   *New York and Pennsylvania.*

784. If your nose itches, it means you 'll
                    See a stranger,
                    Kiss a fool,
                    Or be in danger.
                    Peabody, Mass.

785. To sneeze at the table indicates a stranger.
                    Peabody, Mass.

786. To sneeze before breakfast is a sign you will have a caller before night.   *Eastern Massachusetts.*

787. Sneeze before you eat,
                    See a stranger before you sleep.
                    Cape Breton.

788. As many times as you sneeze before breakfast, so many calls will you have before tea (or bed-time).

789. If you sneeze on Saturday, you will have company on Sunday.
                    Massachusetts.

790. Water spilled on the doorstep means a stranger.
                    Ohio.

791. To slop water near a door is a sign of a stranger.
                    Peabody, Mass.

792. A sudden shower of sparks from the fire betokens a visitor.
                    Cape Breton.

793. When you see the soot burning in the back of the chimney, it is a sign of your being visited by a stranger.   *Alabama.*

794. If you crock your knuckles, company will come.
                                                 Massachusetts.

CHAPTER XII.

CURES.

AMULETS.

795. GREEN glass beads worn about the neck will prevent or cure erysipelas. *Chestertown, Md.*

796. Gold beads were formerly a protection against the " King's Evil " (scrofula), and nearly every maiden and matron wore ample strings of beautiful large beads. *Adams, Mass.*

797. Gold beads worn about the neck will cure sore throat. *Windham, Me.*

798. Gold beads worn about the throat were thought to cure or or prevent goître. *Northern Ohio.*

799. A string of gold beads is still held to be a preventive of quinsy, sore throats, and so on. *New Hampshire.*

800. A string of gold beads worn on the neck will cure or prevent quinsy. *Prince Edward Island.*

801. Red beads about the neck cure nose-bleed. *Cazenovia, N. Y.*

802. For nose-bleed wear a red bean on a white string round the neck. *Bedford, Mass.*

803. A black silk cord about the neck cures croup. *Cazenovia, N. Y.*

804. A key worn hanging about the neck by a string prevents nose-bleed. *Central Maine.*

805. Wearing brown paper on the chest will cure sea-sickness. *Newton, Mass., and Chestertown, Md.*

806. Tie a piece of black ribbon around a child's neck, and it will prevent croup. *Waltham, Mass.*

807. Brass earrings or rings are thought by negroes to keep away rheumatism. *Alabama.*

808. To cure rheumatism, wear a brass ring on the finger.
Boston, Mass.

809. Wearing brass rings will prevent cramp.   *Alabama.*

810. A brass ring worn on the finger will cure rheumatism.
Chestertown, Md. (negro).

811. Sailors wear gold earrings for weak eyes or to strengthen the sight.   *Brookline, Mass.*

812. A common custom among negroes is to wear a leather strap about the wrist as a cure for rheumatism, sprains, etc., and to give strength.   *Chestertown, Md. (negro).*

813. As a cure for nose-bleed, tie a string about the little finger.
Cape Breton.

814. A leather string commonly worn around the neck is supposed to prevent whooping-cough.   *Chestertown, Md.*

815. A red string tied about the waist cures nausea or sea-sickness.   *Massachusetts.*

CHARM.

816. To keep fire always burning on the hearth will prevent cholera among chickens.   *Alabama.*

817. If a fish-hook pierces the hand, stick it three times into wood, in the name of the Trinity, to prevent festering or other evil consequences.   *Newfoundland.*

818. If you scratch yourself with a rusty nail, stick the nail immediately into hard wood, and it will prevent lockjaw.
Salem, Mass.

819. A man who "stuck a nail in his foot" was told by a neighbor to pull it out, grease it, and hang it up in the "chimbly," otherwise he might have lockjaw.   *New Brunswick.*

820. To cure nose-bleeding, write the person's name on the forehead.   *Newfoundland.*

821. For rheumatism, carry a horseshoe nail in the pocket.
Central New York.

822. To get rid of rheumatism: "You go in de lot an' go up to fence. Den put you breas' on it and say, 'I lef you here, I lef you here,' tree times, den you go 'way and don't you never come back dere no more."   *French Canadian.*

823. To cure fits, the first time the child or person has one, tear off the shirt of the patient and burn it up, and no more fits will return. *Chestertown, Md. (negro).*

824. If you don't want the cramp in your foot, turn your shoes bottom up at night. *Nashua, N. H.*

825. To keep off nightmare, put your shoes at night with the toes pointing away from the bed. *Central New York.*

826. To ward off nightmare, sleep with shears under the pillow. *Central New York.*

827. Nightmare is caused by the nightmare man, a kind of evil spirit, struggling with one. It is prevented by placing a sharp knife under the pillow, and stuffing the keyhole with cotton. *Windham, Me.*

828. Sores can be cured by those who possess magical powers going through certain incantations, which are to be followed by applications of oatmeal and vinegar. *Newfoundland.*

829. For a sty on the eye, take a small piece of paper, rub it on the sty, go across the road three times, and say each time, —

> Sty, sty, go off my eye,
> Go on the first one that passes by.

This is a sure cure in two or three days. *Talladega, Ala.*

830. To cure a sty repeat at a cross-roads, —

> Sty, sty, leave my eye,
> And take the next one that passes by.
> *Massachusetts, Indiana, and California.*

831. Toothache may be cured by conjurers, who apply the finger to the aching tooth, while muttering a charm, or tie a number of knots in a fishing line. *Newfoundland.*

832. Toothache may be cured by a written charm, sealed up and worn around the neck of the afflicted person. The following is a copy of the charm : —

> I 've seen it written a feller was sitten
> On a marvel stone, and our Lord came by,
> And He said to him, " What 's the matter with thee, my man ?"
> And he said, " Got the toothache, Marster,"
> And he said, " Follow me and thee shall have no more toothache."
> *Newfoundland.*

833. For toothache take an eyelash, an eyebrow, trimmings of the finger-nails, and toe-nails of the patient, bore a hole in a beech-tree, and put them in. The sufferer must not see the tree, and it must not be cut down or burned. *Cape Breton.*

834. Treat biliousness by boring three holes in a tree and walking three times around it, saying, "Go away, bilious."
Eastern Shore of Maryland.

835. The most powerful charm is a piece of printed paper called "the letter of Jesus Christ." This, in addition to the well-known letter of Lentulus to the Senate, contains many absurd superstitions, such as the promise of safe delivery in child-bed, and freedom from bodily hurt to those who may possess a copy of it.
Newfoundland.

WATER.

836. Rub the hands with the first snow that falls and you'll not have sore hands all winter. *Winn, Me.*

837. On Ash Wednesday before sunrise dip a pail of water in a running brook (up stream), bottle it, and keep as a cure for anything. *Maine.*

838. Catch the last snow of the season (*e. g.*, in April), melt and put into a bottle. It will cure sore eyes. *Chestertown, Md.*

839. Water made from snow that falls in the month of May will cure sore eyes. *Prince Edward Island.*

840. Rain-water caught the first of June will cure freckles. It will not putrefy. *Massachusetts.*

841. An Indian doctor used for inflammation of the eyes rain-water caught on the third, fourth, and fifth of June. It is said that this will not putrefy. *New Hampshire.*

842. The first water that falls in June is supposed to cure all skin diseases; and I am informed "it is dretful good for the insides, too." *Westford, Mass.*

843. Water in which a blacksmith has cooled his iron is a cure for freckles. *Malden, Mass.*

MISCELLANEOUS.

844. It is believed that "piercing the ear" will cure weak eyes or strengthen the eyes. It is often done to children for this purpose.
Northern Ohio.

845. To cure hiccoughs repeat in one breath the words, —

There was an old woman who lived all alone,
And she was made of skin and bone.
One day to church she went to pray,
And on the ground a man there lay,
And from his head unto his feet
The worms crawled in, the worms crawled out.
Boston, Mass.

846. A variant, —

There was an old woman who lived all alone,
And she was made of skin and bone.
One day to church she went to pray,
And on the ground there lay a man.
And from his head unto his feet
The worms crawled in, the worms crawled out.
The woman to the parson said :
"Shall I be so when I am dead?"
The parson he said "yes."
Portland, Me., Brookline and Deerfield, Mass.

847. For hiccoughs the nurse used to say in a droning, deep, ghostly tone, —

There was an old man an' an old woman,
And they lived in a bottle and eat Bones.
Brookline, Mass.

848. Other somewhat general remedies for hiccoughs are to munch a spoonful of sugar, to scare the one troubled with hiccoughs by some startling announcement or accusation, as, "See, you've torn your dress!" or, "How did you break my vase?" etc. Another custom is to steadily point a finger at the hiccougher, or to make him hold up his arm and shake it.

849. To cure hiccoughs, slowly take nine sips of water.
Prince Edward Island and Northern Ohio.

850. Another cure for hiccoughs is as follows : Put the thumb up against the lower lip, with the fingers under the chin, and say, "hiccup, hiccup, over my thumb," nine times. *Northern Ohio.*

851. A cure for hiccoughs : Try for a long time to make the edges of the thumb-nails meet at the end.   *Chestertown, Md.*

852. Think of the one you love best, to cure hiccoughs.
          Prince Edward Island.

853. For chapped lips kiss the middle rail of a five-railed fence.
          Bernardston, Mass.

854. To relieve coughing or strangling, put a pair of scissors down inside the back of your dress.   *Prince Edward Island.*

855. Chew brown paper as a cure for nose-bleed.
          Eastern Massachusetts.

856. For nose-bleed, put a key down the back.

857. For nose-bleed, hold up the right arm.

858. For nose-bleed, place a wad of paper between the upper lip and the gum.

859. You can keep from crying as you peel onions if you keep the mouth closed.   *Northern Ohio.*

860. Hold, by the points, two needles between your teeth, as you peel onions, and you will not cry.   *Prince Edward Island.*

861. Hold a needle between your teeth with the point out, while peeling onions, and you 'll not cry, *i. e.*, will not feel the smart.

862. You will not cry in peeling onions if you hold a bit of bread in the mouth.
          Prince Edward Island, Cambridge, Mass. (Irish).
Or, put the bread on the point of the knife.   *Maine.*

863. You will not cry in peeling onions if you let the faucet be open so the water will run.   *Cambridge, Mass.*

864. To bring up the palate when it drops and tickles the root of the tongue, take a wisp of hair on the crown of the head and tie it up very tight.   *Chestertown, Md.*

865. Rubbing a sty with a gold ring will cure it.
          Prince Edward Island.
866. Cure a sty by rubbing it with a wedding ring.
          General.

867. A sty in the eye is cured by rubbing a gold ring on the eye three mornings with a sign of the cross. *Labrador.*

868. A pebble in the mouth will ease thirst.

Brookline, Mass.

869. A sore throat may be cured by binding about the neck on going to bed one of the stockings which the patient has been wearing (no other one will do).

Somewhat general in the United States.

870. To cure the sore throat, take three handfuls of ashes with your left hand, put into your left stocking, and bind it around your throat. *Mattawamkeag, Me.*

871. To burn the "little nerve" in the ear will cure the toothache forever. *Northern Ohio.*

CHAPTER XIII.

WARTS.

CAUSES.

872. BLOOD from the warts on a cow's bag coming in contact with a person's hands will cause warts to appear on them.
New Hampshire.

873. Blood from a wart, especially if applied to the tongue, will cause warts to appear. *New Jersey.*

874. To count another person's warts will cause them to appear on you. *General in the United States.*

875. If one counts stars while lying on his back, he will have as many warts as he has counted stars.
New York and Trenton, N. J.

876. To drink the water in which eggs have been boiled will cause internal warts. *Miramichi, N. B.*

877. Washing the hands in water in which eggs have been boiled causes warts to grow. *Cape Breton and Eastern Massachusetts.*

878. Warts are caused by touching the white of an egg.
Salem, Mass.

879. To touch the jelly-fish will cause warts.
Halifax, N. S., and parts of Eastern New England.

880. Touching the excrescences that sometimes appear on trees will cause warts on the hand of the person who touches them.
New England.

881. The handling of large species of toadstool, sometimes popularly called "wart-toadstool," will cause warts to grow on the part of the hand coming in contact with it. *New Hampshire.*

882. The handling of a toad will cause warts to appear.
General in the United States.

CURES.

883. To cure a wart, grease it with stolen bacon, and hide the latter.

884. Split a bean and put one half on the wart, one half in the ground, and at the end of the week dig up the latter ; place on the wart with the other half ; bury again, and this will cure the wart.
Greenfield, Mass.

885. Beans rubbed on a wart and thrown in the well will cure a wart.
Maine.

886. Rub a white bean on the warts, wrap it in paper, and throw it on the road ; whoever picks it up will get the warts.
Connecticut.

887. If you find an old bone in the field, rub the wart with it, then lay it down exactly as you found it.   The wart will be cured.
Maine.

888. If a person has warts, he should rub them with a bone, and after replacing the bone they are said to leave.   *Alabama.*

889. Rub a wart with the yellow milky juice of celandine (*Chelidonium majus*).
Massachusetts.

890. The juice of "wild celandine" (*Impatiens fulva*) is used as a wart cure.
Franconia, N. H.

891. Dandelion juice will cure warts.   *Revere Beach, Mass.*

892. The milky juice of the *Euphorbia hypericifolia* (and other small prostrate Euphorbias) is thought to be a sure cure for warts.
Northern Ohio.

893. The milky juice of the common cypress spurge (*Euphorbia Cyparissias*) will cure warts.

894. The juice of the common large milk-weeds (Asclepias) will cure warts.
Massachusetts.

895. The juice of the "milk-thistles" (Sonchus) will cure warts.
Prince Edward Island.

896. The milky juice of the Osage orange is used as a wart-cure.
Southern Ohio.

897. The first time a person has seen your wart, if it is rubbed with fresh cream by that person, the wart will surely go away.
Bruynswick, N. Y.

898. Rub a wart with a stolen dish-cloth, and then hide or bury
the latter. As it decays, the wart will disappear.

General in the United States.

899. Rub the wart with a stolen dish-cloth, and secrete the dish-
cloth until it becomes mouldy and decays, then the wart is cured.

Bucks Co., Pa.

900. To cure a wart: Draw a blade across it, and then draw the
knife across a sweet apple-tree. *Lawrence, Mass.*

901. Warts are cured by stealing pork from the family barrel of
salted pork, rubbing the warts with it, and throwing it into the road.
The person who picks it up gets the warts.

Bruynswick, N. Y.

902. Sell your warts for money, throw the money away anywhere,
but on your own land. Whoever picks up the money gets also the
warts. *Springfield, Mass.*

903. To cure warts : Cut your finger-nails and put them in the
knothole of a tree ; then stop up the hole, wishing the warts on to
some one else. *Connecticut.*

904. Make a wart bleed, and put the blood on a penny, throw
the latter away, and the finder will get the wart.

905. Cut up an onion, rub the wart with each slice, and bury all
the slices. *Bucks Co., Pa.*

906. Split a pea and rub the wart with both pieces, make a wish
that some person shall get the wart, throw one piece over one shoulder and the other over the other (into the river), and the wart will
go to the person wished. *Miramichi, N. B.*

907. If you rub your warts with a pebble, wrap the pebble in paper,
and throw it away; the person who picks it up will have them come
to him. Or, should you label the paper with some one's name and
throw it away, the warts will go to the person whose name you have
written. *New England.*

908. Take a green, mossy pebble, wrap it up, tie it, and throw
it away. The finder will catch the wart which you had.

Rhode Island.

909. Take as many pebbles as there are warts. Rub them on the
warts. Roll them in paper and throw them away. The finder takes
the warts. *Boxford, Mass.*

910. Go out of doors, count three, stop and pick up the stone nearest to your toe. Wrap it up in a paper, and throw it away. The one that picks it up will get the warts. *Providence, R. I.*

911. Count out secretly as many stones as you have warts, tie in a rag, and throw them where they can't be seen.
Massachusetts.

912. If you have warts, walk nine steps backward with your eyes shut, having just picked up a pebble with which rub the wart, and throw it away. *Fort Worth, Tex.*

913. To cure warts, wash the hands in warm pig's blood.
Nova Scotia.

914. Steal as many pins as you have warts, wrap them in paper, and throw them in the road : the warts will attack whoever picks up the paper, and leave you. *Bruynswick, N. Y.*

915. Run a pin through the wart, and put the pin in the road ; the finder gets the wart. *Missouri.*

916. Rub warts with the head of a pin ; hide the latter and do not look for it, or tie a knot in a string, lay it away, and do not look for it, and the warts will disappear. *Western New York.*

917. Take a potato and rub it over the wart, then wrap the potato in a piece of paper and throw it away. The one who finds it will have the wart. *Maine.*

918. Rub the wart with a cotton rag, spit on the rag and hide it under a water-board (a wooden gutter used as a duct for rain-water off the roof of a house), where the water will drip on it. The whole operation must be kept secret. *Kansas.*

919. Rub the wart with rock-salt till it bleeds, and throw a lump of salt in the fire ; if it crackles and snaps out of the fire, the wart will get well ; if not, not. *Central Maine.*

920. Binding a slug (*Limax*) on a wart will cure it.
Cazenovia, N. Y.

921. Rub the warts with the sole of your shoe ; as the leather wears away, the warts depart. *Springfield, Mass.*

922. When a person wishes to remove warts from his hand, cut as many notches on a stick as you have warts, and standing on a bridge,

throw the stick over your left shoulder, and turn your head ; they will go off before you leave the bridge. *Alabama.*

923. Cut notches in a stick to the number of warts you have, and then bury the stick. *Massachusetts.*

924. Some pretend to remove warts by "touching with the sharp point of a stick and rubbing them in the notch of another stick; then if the patient tells of it, they will come back. *Alabama.*

925. Take as many joints of oat or wheat straw as a person has warts, and burn them under a stone. As the joints rot, the warts disappear. This is to be done by another for you.

Cape Breton.

926. Rub saliva on the wart, tie a string around the hand so that the knot comes on the wart. Take off the string and hide in a hollow stump. *Southern Indiana.*

927. Kill a toad, and put its blood on the wart. The warts will go away in three weeks. *Marquette, Mich.*

928. Warts are cured by tying a knot in a string for every wart, and putting under the eaves of the house. The warts go as the string rots. *Ohio.*

929. Warts may be cured by applying to them water standing in the hollow of an oaken stump. *Boxford, Mass., and Ohio.*

CHAPTER XIV.

WEATHER.

COLD.

930. As the days begin to lengthen,
So the cold begins to strengthen.
Northeastern United States and Canada.

931. Fire spitting sparks means cold weather. *Patten, Me.*

932. If the fire burns well, it is coming cold weather.
General in the United States.

933. Fog in winter is always succeeded by cold and wind.

934. Plenty of hawberries foretell a "hard winter," *i. e.*, they are to serve as a store of food for birds. *Canada.*

935. Cold weather comes after the wind has blown over the oat stubble. *Pennsylvania.*

DAYS AND TIMES.

936. The first Tuesday after the new moon settles the weather for that quarter. *Newfoundland.*

937. If it is a fair sunset Friday night, it will rain before Monday.
Massachusetts.

938. If it storms on a Friday, it will storm again before the next Monday. *Massachusetts and New York.*

939. If the sun sets clear Friday night, it will not rain before Monday night ; but if it sets in a cloud, it will rain before Monday night. *Boston, Mass.*

940. The weather of the last Friday in the month governs the next month. *Cambridge, Mass.*

941. There will be sun during some part of Saturday the year through. *Brookline, Mass.*

942. If it rains the last Saturday or the first Sunday in a month, it will rain the three following Sundays. *Maine.*

943. The sun shines some part of every Saturday in the year but one. *New England.*

944. Saturday's moon comes seven years too soon, and denotes bad weather. *Newfoundland.*

945. Sunday's sail
Will never fail.
Topsail Bay, N. F.

946. Weather is apt to repeat itself in the following week, *i. e.,* there will be a run of wet Sundays or fine Tuesdays, etc.
Brookline, Mass.

947. The first seven days of January indicate the first seven months of the year. Mild days, mild months, etc. *Nova Scotia.*

948. If March comes in like a lamb, it goes out like a lion, and *vice versa.* *General in the United States.*

949. The corn is planted when the Baltimore orioles appear, or when the first green is noticed on the oak-trees. *Milton, Mass.*

950. A dry May and a wet June
Make the farmer whistle a merry tune.
Franklin Centre, R. I.

951. It rains often on July fourth. That is due to the firing of cannon, etc. *General in the United States.*

952. If there is a wet September, there will be a next summer's drouth ; no crops and famine. *California.*

953. If it rains on Easter, it will rain seven Sundays thereafter.
Hennepin, Ill.

954. A green Christmas makes a full churchyard, or
A green Christmas makes a fat graveyard.
General in the United States.

955. The twelve days at Christmas govern the weather of the months of the coming year. *Eastern Massachusetts.*

956. The twelve days at Christmas time make the almanac for the year. *Massachusetts.*

957. It is a general notion that a cold winter is followed by a hot summer, and *vice versa.*

958. It always rains while the Cadets are in camp.
Eastern Massachusetts.

959. It always rains during May meetin's. *Boston, Mass.*

960. It always rains during a cattle-show. *Deerfield, Mass.*

961. Women "cruising," *i. e.,* visiting about on "pot-days," especially Sundays, Tuesdays, and Thursdays, when people have their best dinner (usually pork and cabbage) in the pot, is a sign of bad weather. But it is also said that it is a sign of mild weather.
Newfoundland and Labrador.

FAIR OR FOUL.

962. Of a change : —
>Long looked for
>Long last,
>Short notice,
>Soon past.
>>*Brookline, Mass.*

963. From twelve till two
>Tells what the day will do.
>>*New England.*

964. If it rains before seven
>It will drip before eleven.
>>*Eastern Maine.*

965. If it rain before seven
>It will quit before eleven.
>>*Prince Edward Island and, Maine, Massachusetts,*
>>*and Northern Ohio.*

966. If a storm clears off in the night, pleasant weather will last but a few hours. *Northern Ohio.*

967. In uncertain or threatening weather it is said that if you can see a piece of blue sky big enough to make a pair of breeches, it will clear off. *Maine, Massachusetts, and Northern Ohio.*

968. Variant: If you can see enough blue sky in the west to make an old woman's apron, it will clear off. *Eastern Maine.*

969. Clocks and watches tick louder before mild weather.
Scilly Cove, N. F.

√ 970. Cobwebs on the grass are a sign of fair weather.
General in the United States.

971. If every dish is cleaned at a given meal, then look for fair weather the following day. *Pennsylvania Germans.*

972. Fog lying in valleys is a sign of a "civil" day.
Bay Roberts, N. F.

973. If hoar frost remains after sunrise, the day will be fine; if not, the day will be wet. *Scilly Cove, N. F.*

974. A load of hay passing means fair weather.
Massachusetts.

975. Rainbow in the morning,
Sailors take warning ;
Rainbow at night,
Sailor's delight.
General in Canada and the United States.

976. A rainbow is a sign of showers. *Prince Edward Island.*

√ 977. Rain falling while the sun is shining indicates more showers. *Prince Edward Island and Northern Ohio.*

978. Rain falling while the sun shines is a sign it will rain next day. *Methuen, Mass.*

979. Rain falling while the sun is shining means that the devil is beating his wife with a codfish. *General in the United States.*

980. Thunder in the morning,
All the day storming ;
Thunder at night
Is the sailor's delight.

√ 981. Red at night
Sailor's delight ;
Red in the morning,
Sailors take warning.
Maine and Eastern Massachusetts.

982. Evening red and morning gray
Will speed the traveler on his way.
Evening gray and morning red
Will bring the rain upon his head.
Massachusetts, New York, and Ohio.

983. Evening red and morning gray,
You 'll surely have a pleasant day.
New York.

984. Red sun, hot day to-morrow.

985. High wind at dawn is a sign of a "civil" (calm) day.
Newfoundland.

986. Sun's "hounds" (a sort of halo) before the sun denote dirty weather; after the sun, denote fine weather.   *Scilly Cove, N. F.*

In Prince Edward Island and the United States these halos are called "sun-dogs," and are said to be a sign of coming rain.

987. Much snow during the winter denotes good crops next year.
New Harbor, N. F.

988. If the stars are scarce, big, and dull, it portends mild weather in winter. If large and bright, it portends frost in winter.
Newfoundland.

989. Stars twinkling are a sign of bad weather.
Labrador and New Harbor, N. F.

MOON.

990. When the moon is on the back, it denotes weather wet or mild; when on the end, it denotes frost.   *Newfoundland.*

991. Should the new moon lie on its back, it is a sign it will be dry that month, for the moon would hold water. The Indian says the hunter can hang his powder-horn upon it. But should the new moon stand vertically, it will be a wet month, for the moon will not hold water, and the powder-horn will slip off. Very many, however, reverse these signs.   *New England, New York, and Ohio.*

992. The Indians told the first settlers that if the moon lay well on her back, so that a powder-horn could be hung on the end, the weather during that moon will be dry.   *Nova Scotia.*

993. The moon changing in the west denotes that fine weather will prevail during that moon.   *Bay Roberts, N. F.*

994. If the moon changes near midnight there will be fine weather. The nearer to midnight, the finer the weather.
Conception Bay, N. F.

995. A disk or ring around the moon indicates bad weather (rain or snow).   *Newfoundland.*

996. A circle round the moon means rain. In some localities the number of stars inside the circle denotes the number of days until it will rain.   *Prince Edward Island; general in the United States.*

997.   Where there is a ring around the moon, whichever way the ring opens, the wind will blow in.   If it does not open there will be fine weather.   The bigger the ring the nearer the bad weather.
Trinity Bay, N. F.

998. If the new moon is of light color, there will be a frost ; if it is red, it will be mild for a month.   *Bay Roberts, N. F.*

999. The weather of the new moon governs the month's weather.
Newfoundland.

1000. The weather of the new moon governs the first quarter and after that remains the same ; therefore it governs the first half.
Conception Bay, N. F.

1001. The moon being red near midnight, with blunted corners or horns, portends mild weather that month.   If the corners are white and sharp, there will be frosty weather.   *Conception Bay, N. F.*

1002. If there is a star before the moon, the weather will be calm ; if the star is behind the moon, the weather will be stormy.
New Harbor, N. F.

RAIN.

1003. A load of barrels foretells wet weather.
Eastern Massachusetts.

1004. When the Brothers (Catholic theological students) turn out in a procession it will rain soon.   *Baltimore, Md.*

1005. When a great many women are seen on the street, it will rain next day.   *Bedford, Mass.*

1006. When you blow out the candle, if the fire on the wick burns bright, it means a fair day on the morrow ; if it dies down on being blown out, it indicates a rainy day.   *Plymouth, O.*

1007. When long cirrus clouds or " cow's tails " are seen, it means rain.   *Lewisburg, Pa.*

1008. Cobwebs on the grass for three mornings running are a sign of wet.

1009. If there is no dew on the grass at night, it will rain the next day.   *General in the United States.*

1010. Conjurers can stop rain by throwing up clods of dirt.
Alabama.

1011. Fog on the hill
Brings water to the mill.
Fog on the moor
Brings the sun to the door.

New York.

1012. A fog from the hills
Brings water to the mills.
A fog from the sea
Drives all the rain away.

Prince Edward Island.

1013. Fog on the hill
Brings water to the mill.
Fog in the vale,
Catch all the water in a pail.

Massachusetts.

1014. Three foggy mornings and then a rain.

Massachusetts.

1015. It will rain within twenty-four hours of a hoar frost.

Deerfield, Mass.

1016. When the glass sweats, it is the sign of rainy weather.

Alabama.

1017. If the ground is black, it means rain. *Peabody, Mass.*

1018. To wear your husband's hat is a sign of rain.

Massachusetts.

1019. Talking of horses is a sign of rain. *Labrador.*

1020. Mackerel sky
Five miles high
Lets the earth
Go three days dry.

Miller's River, Mass.

1021. Mackerel sky,
Rain by and by.

Massachusetts.

1022. A mackerel sky is a sign of a storm.

Prince Edward Island.

1023. Mackerel sky,
Rain is nigh.

or

Mackerel sky,
Rain to-morrow.

Brookline, Mass.

1024. Mackerel sky
Three days high
Never leaves the earth
Three days dry.
Massachusetts.

1025. Mackerel's back and the mare's tails
Make lofty ships carry low sails.
Newburyport, Mass.

1026. Mackerel sky, horse's tail,
Make the sailor draw his sail.
Brookline, Mass.

1027. Mackerel sky,
Wind blow high.
Canada.

1028. Mackerel sky,
Twenty-four hours dry.
Salem, Mass.

1029. Open and shet,
Sign of wet.
Maine and Massachusetts.

1030. Open and shet,
Sign of more wet.
Massachusetts.

1031. Open and shet,
Kind o' wet.
Massachusetts.

1032. If raindrops linger on the pane,
There will be further rain.

1033. Raindrops falling on a river, etc., and raising large bubbles, mean a heavy fall of rain and a flood.

1034. If you can see the reflection of the building, etc., in puddles in the street, it will rain inside of twelve hours. *Salem, Mass.*

1035. When the rain dries up quickly from puddles, it will rain again soon. *Mattawamkeag, Me.*

1036. The rope becoming slack denotes that rain is coming.
Placentia Bay, N. F.

1037. Sparks on the bottom of the tea-kettle mean rain.
Patten, Me.

1038. The sun drawing water means rain.
General in the United States.

1039. When the sun sets in a bank of clouds, there will soon be rain.
Alabama.

1040. It is believed that a rain may be stopped by putting one umbrella or more out in the rain. The longer left the better.
New Orleans, La. (negro).

1041. Water boiling over out of a kettle is a sign of rain.
Labrador.

1042. Water boiling away quickly from the kettle is a sign of rain.
Newfoundland; general in the United States.

1043. The same, however, is also said to be a sign of mild weather.
Bay Roberts, N. F.

1044. To eat or sing in the water-closet betokens rain the next day.
Eastern Massachusetts.

1045. Water low in wells is a sign of rain.
Placentia Bay, N. F.

1046. Whistle to bring rain.
Newfoundland.

1047. When you hear a distant locomotive whistle, it is a sign of rain.
Alabama.

1048. Comes the rain before the wind,
Then your topsail you must mind.
Comes the wind before the rain,
Haul your topsails up again.
Cape Cod, Mass.

1049. In northerly squalls : —

If the rain comes before the wind,
'T is time your topsail to take in ;
If the wind before the rain,
You may hoist your topsail up again.
Labrador.

WIND AND STORM.

1050. A broom falling across the doorway, or chairs set crosswise, is the sign of a storm.
Stratham, N. H.

1051. If a cloud and wind are coming, the wind will last.
Trinity Bay, N. F.

1052. If a cloud looks as if it had been picked by a hen,
Get ready to reef your topsails then.
Mansfield, O.

1053. Clothes hanging about the rigging will bring wind.
Newfoundland.

1054. Blue blazes in a coal fire mean a storm.
Eastern Massachusetts.

1055. When wood on the fire makes a peculiar hissing noise, it is said "to tread snow," and there will soon be a storm.
Salem, Mass.

1056. If the stove-lids get red-hot when the fire is first made, it is a sure sign of a storm of some kind. *Cambridge, Mass.*

1057. If the vessel is becalmed, throw a halfpenny overboard to buy wind. *Harbor Grace, N. F.*

1058. If the halyard lies against the mast, the wind will increase.
Newfoundland.

1059. Sticking a knife in the mainmast produces wind.
Conception Bay, N. F.

1060. Table-knives turning blue denote that a northeast wind is coming. *Placentia Bay, N. F.*

1061. Strange lights at sea are seen before a northeast gale.
Newfoundland.

1062. To see Northern Lights denotes that south wind and storm will come inside of forty-eight hours. *Massachusetts.*

1063. If the fall "line storm" clears off warm, it signifies that storms through that fall and winter will clear away with mild weather, *i. e.*, the way in which the storm closes at the autumnal equinox will rule the weather following storms until the vernal equinox storm. Then the same saying applies to the "line-storm" of March, and the spring and summer *after* storms is foretold.

The contrary would happen if cool weather followed the line storm. *Weathersfield, Vt.*

1064. In the fall, if the sky is red in the west at sunset, a gale is coming from the northeast. *Newfoundland.*

1065. If a red sky turn gray, the wind will be north.
Newfoundland.

1066. First rise after low
Foretells stronger blow.

1067. Sailors putting the end of the sheet overboard will bring wind. Hitting with it three times across the thwart stops the wind.
Topsail Bay, N. F.

1068. The day of the month of the first snowstorm indicates the number of storms in the year. *Eastern Massachusetts.*

1069. If the stars are remarkably clear and bright, it is likely there will be a storm the next day.

1070. Stars in a circle around the moon foretell a storm in the same number of days as there are stars.

Maine, Massachusetts, and New York.

1071. Stars shooting about portend wind.

Heart's Delight, N. F.

1072. A shooting star shows that wind is coming from the direction toward which it goes. *Conception Bay, New Harbor, N. F.*

1073. If stars are in thick patches before twelve at night, it is a sign that wind will come next day from that quarter.

Heart's Delight, Trinity Bay, N. F.

1074. For the sun to rise and go into a cloud means a storm.

Massachusetts.

1075. If the sun sets in a bank, the wind will be in the "western bank." *Bay Roberts, N. F.*

1076. If the bottom of the tea-kettle is white when taken from the stove, it indicates a snowstorm. *Peabody, Mass.*

1077. The sun "getting up water" denotes wind and dirty weather. *Scilly Cove, N. F.*

1078. Whistle for a breeze. *Universal among sailors.*

1079. Whistling of wind in blocks aloft is a sign of a heavy storm.

Conception Bay, N. F.

CHAPTER XV.

MOON.

DIVINATION.

1080. REPEAT, looking at the new moon the first time you see it, —

> New moon, true moon, tell unto me
> Who my true love is to be;
> The color of his hair, the clothes he is to wear,
> And when he 'll be married to me.
>
> *Mansfield, O.*

1081. On first seeing the new moon, hold any small object in the hand while you repeat, —

> New moon, true moon, reveal to me
> Who my true love shall be;
> The color of his hair, the clothes he shall wear,
> And the day that we shall wedded be.

Put the object — handkerchief, pebble, or what not — under your pillow at night, and you will dream of your future husband.

> *Prince Edward Island.*

1082. New moon, moon,
> Hail unto thee!
> In my sleep upon my bed,
> May the one I am to wed
> In my dreams smile on me.
>
> *Middleboro', Mass.*

1083. If you see the new moon over the right shoulder, take three steps backward and repeat, —

> New moon, true moon, true and bright,
> If I have a lover let me dream of him to-night.
> If I 'm to marry far, let me hear a bird cry;
> If I 'm to marry near, let me hear a cow low;
> If I 'm never to marry, let me hear a hammer knock.

One of these sounds is always heard.　　　　　*Tennessee.*

1084. Say to the new moon over your right shoulder, —

> New moon, new moon. come play your part,
> And tell me who 's my own sweetheart ;
> The color of his hair, the clothes he shall wear,
> And on what day he shall appear.

Then dream.   *Massachusetts.*

1085. The first time you see the moon in the New Year, look at
it and say, —

> Whose table shall I spread ?
> For whom make the bed ?
> Whose name shall I carry ?
> And whom shall I marry ?

Then think of one you would like to marry, and go your way.
Ask some question of the first person you meet, and if the answer is
affirmative, it indicates that you will marry your choice ; if negative,
it means you will not.

Told by a Norwegian girl in Eastern Massachusetts.

1086. Rest a mirror on the head and look at the new moon in it ;
as many moons as you see mean the number of months before marriage.

1087. When it is new moon, take out a stocking, and as you knit
repeat, —

> This knot I knit
> To know the thing I know not yet,
> This night that I may see
> Who my husband is to be,
> How he goes and what he wears,
> And what he does all days and years.

Nashua, N. H.

1088. Look over the right shoulder at the new moon, and count
nine stars, pick up whatever is under your right foot, such as a stick,
pebble, or what not ; put it under your pillow, and you will dream of
whoever is to be your husband.   *Deer Isle, Me.*

1089. When you see the moon, say, —

> I see the moon and the moon sees me,
> And the moon sees somebody that I want to see.

Massachusetts.

1090. New moon, true moon, true and trusty,
> Tell me who my true love must be.

Pennsylvania.

1091. Wish the first time you see the moon, and your wish will come true.　　　　*General in the United States and Canada.*

1092. Bow to the new moon seven times the first time you see it, and you 'll get a present, or wish and you will get your wish.
New England.

1093. If you shake your dress at the new moon, you will get a new one.　　　　*Alabama.*

FORTUNE.

1094. The moon seen over the right shoulder brings good luck; over the left shoulder, ill luck.　　　　*General in the United States.*

1095. If you should see the moon over your left shoulder, and should without speaking turn round and look at it over your right shoulder, your ill luck will disappear, and you will be as well off as if you had seen it over your right shoulder first.
Maine and Massachusetts.

1096. It is bad luck to look at the moon over your right shoulder. If through mistake you should look at it over your right, face around, take three steps backward with your hands clasped behind, and then look at it over the left shoulder.　　　　*Alabama.*

1097. If you see the moon square in the face, you 'll have a fall.
Nashua, N. H.

1098. See the moon over the left shoulder,
You will have a fall (tumble).
Bedford, Mass.

1199. If you have money in the pocket when you first see the new moon, turn it over, and you 'll have plenty all the rest of the month.　　　　*Stratham, N. H.*

1100. If you have money in your pocket the first time you see the new moon, and it is seen over your right shoulder, you will have money all the year.　　　　*Nashua, N. H., and Massachusetts.*

1101. Take out money and shake it in the hand on first seeing the new moon; it will increase your wealth.　　　　*Miramichi, N. B.*

1102. Look at the new moon through a ring, wish something while doing so, and your wish will come true.　　　　*Alabama.*

1103. If you first see the new moon with full hands, that is, with busy hands, you will be busy, full of work, all the month; if idle, the reverse.

1104. See the new moon through a glass,
See sorrow while it lasts.
Deer Isle, Me., and Salem, Mass.

1105. If you see the new moon through trees or brush, you will have trouble that month.　　*General in the United States.*

1106. If you see the new moon full in front, you will meet your lover within the week.

1107. If you see the new moon face on, you will go headlong through the month.　　*Salem, Mass.*

1108. Moon full face,
Open disgrace.
Portland, Me.

1109. One who chances to have a cup in his hand when he first sees the new moon is destined to wait on the sick until another new moon appears.　　*Alabama.*

MOONLIGHT.

1110. Some say you can see the man's axe and dog in the moon.
New Brunswick.

1111. If the moon shines in your face as you lie in the bed at night, you 'll die inside of a year.　　*Central Maine.*

1112. It is a general belief that it is dangerous to sleep with the moon shining on the face. (If the moon shines on fish, they will spoil.)

1113. Horses will be cured of any one of several diseases if you will insert a bit of silver — a dime is the favorite coin — in the part affected; but it is imperative that you do this by the "light of the moon."　　*Clover Bend, Ark.*

WAX AND WANE.

1114. Set out cabbages in the new of the moon to make them head up well, and gather apples in the new of the moon to make them keep well.　Plant potatoes in the old of the moon.
Mitchell Co., N. C.

1115. Plant flowers in the increase of the moon.
Pennsylvania.

1116. Be careful as to the phase of the moon when felling timber.
General in the United States.

1117. If brush and thistles are cut down in the full moon in August when the sign is in the heart, they will never grow again.
Copied from an agricultural paper.

1118. Grass cut when the moon is waning will not "spend well."
New England.

1119. If cut when it is waxing, the hay weighs and spends well.
New England.

1120. Plant peas and potatoes in the increase of the moon.
Miramichi, N. B.

1121. Seeds should be sown when the moon is new. This custom is still more or less observed. Corn should be planted at this time.
Boston, Mass.

1122. Plant seed the first three days after the moon changes.
Alabama.

1123. Plant potatoes "in the dark of the moon," so the potatoes will root and yield well. *Mansfield, O.*

1124. The full moon is the time to cut alders, spruce, or other undergrowth, because the roots then die quickly without sprouting.
Nova Scotia.

1125. Shingle the roof in the decrease of the moon, so the shingles will lie flat ("go down"). Else they may warp and rise up.
Mansfield, O.

1126. If a farmer lays a rail fence by the light of the moon, it will be stronger and last longer than if it was laid in the daytime.
Western New York and parts of Massachusetts.

1127. Kill any animal for meat on the increase of the moon, and it will increase in the pot. Kill it on the wane of the moon, and it will shrink in the pot. *General in the United States.*

1128. If hogs are butchered on a rising tide, the pork will not shrink in the pan. *Massachusetts.*

1129. You must never kill cattle or pigs, or even wild game, by the "dark of the moon;" it is most unlucky, and the meat will come to no good. *Clover Bend, Ark.*

1130. If you wean a calf at the time of the full moon, it will make less fuss. You must n't wean it when the sign is in the belly, or it will never grow fat. Pursue the same course with a pig, or it will squeal. *Western Massachusetts.*

1131. To make hair grow, cut it in the new of the moon.

N. F., N. B., N. S., Me., Mass., and Talladega, Ala.

1132. Cut hair the first Friday in the new moon, if you wish it to grow. *General in the United States.*

1133. It is the custom for girls to cut their bangs on the forehead when the moon is new. It is supposed to make them grow. This custom is observed by many intelligent young people.

Boston, Mass.

1134. Cut hair in the new moon, bury it in earth near a running brook, and it will make the new hair grow long and abundant.

Maine.

1135. Clean the spring or well during the increase of the moon, so the water will *run in* and fill the spring after it is emptied.

Mansfield, O.

1136. Make soap in the new of the moon. *Talladega, Ala.*

1137. Make soap in the full of the moon.

Prince Edward Island.

1138. Do not marry or move during the wane (decrease) of the moon. *Mansfield, O.*

1139. To take away warts, steal a dish-rag out of the house, without anybody's knowledge, and go out of doors in the first of the moon, rub the dish-rag on the wart, and say: "Here, new moon! take away my new wart." Then throw the dish-rag away where no one can find it, and tell nobody. *Talladega, Ala.*

1140. To cure warts, go out of doors when the moon is new, take up a handful of mud, looking at the moon all the time, and rub on the wart. *Holderness, N. H.*

CHAPTER XVI.

SUN.

DOMESTIC AND MECHANICAL OPERATIONS.

1141. To make good bread, stir it with the sun. To make good yeast, make it as near sunrise as possible.   *Northern Ohio.*

1142. If you wish to secure lightness, you must always stir cake and eggs a certain way, that is, the way the sun goes.
Kittery, Me., Nashua, N. H., Eastern Massachusetts, and Southern Michigan.

1143. Eggs and cake are commonly beaten and butter made by stirring sunwise.   *Newfoundland.*

1144. To make cake light, it must always be stirred the same way.   *Dalton, Mass., and Alabama.*

1145. In cooking soft custard, the stirring must be continued throughout in the direction in which it was begun; otherwise the custard will turn to whey.   *Eastern Massachusetts.*

1146. If, after turning the crank of a churn for a while with the sun, you change and turn the other way, it will undo all the churning you have done.   *Ferrisburgh, Vt.*

1147. Ice cream will not freeze rightly unless the crank is turned the right way.   *Concord, Mass.*

1148. In making lye soap, if you stir it backward it will turn back to lye.   *Warren Co., N. Y., and Alabama.*

1149. In melting sugar for taffy, stir always one way, or it will grain.   *Allston, Mass.*

1150. In greasing the wheels of a carriage, always begin at a certain wheel and go round in a set way.   *Peabody, Mass.*

CURES.

1151. In rubbing for rheumatism, etc., rub from left to right (sunwise).
Concord, Mass.

1152. Ringworm may be killed by moistening the finger in the mouth and rubbing sunwise around the diseased spot.
Central Maine.

1153. To rub for "sweeney." Rub the diseased part of the horse's shoulder with a corn-cob with the sun every third morning.
Northern Ohio.

1154. Rub a corn, a wen, etc., with the sun if by day, with the moon if by night. The sun or moon will draw all the pain away. Related by a Pennsylvania German. *Northern Ohio.*

1155. To cure a curb in a horse, rub it with a bone, at the going down of the sun. *Plymouth, O.*

1156. A "conjurer" can rub away a "rising" (boil) by coming to your bedside about daybreak, before you speak to any one, and rubbing the "rising" for nine successive days. *Talladega, Ala.*

1157. To cure a burn, moisten it with saliva, repeating : —

> As far as the east is from the west,
> Come out fire and go in frost.
> In the name of the Father, Son, and Holy Ghost,
> Come out fire and go in frost.

Blow three times, and rub sunwise three times. To be taught to not more than three persons of the opposite sex.
Eastern Tennessee.

CHAPTER XVII.

DEATH OMENS.

1158. To raise an umbrella in a house is a sign of an approaching death. *Pennsylvania ; somewhat general in the United States.*

1159. To open an umbrella in the house is a sign of ill luck. An action of this sort seriously disturbed a friend of the informant, an American girl of good family. "I would never dare to do that," she said. *Niagara Falls, Ont.*

1160. If a hoe be carried through a house, some one will die before the year is out. *Mansfield, O.*

1161. Carrying through the house a hoe, spade, or axe indicates a death in the family. *Virginia.*

1162. Carry an axe or any iron implement through the house, and some one will soon die. *Southwestern Michigan.*

1163. Death is foretold by the ringing of a bell that cannot otherwise be accounted for. *Southern Ohio.*

1164. When bread, in baking, cracks across the top, it means death. *New Jersey and Ohio.*

1165. Cracks on the top of a loaf of bread indicate the death of a friend. *Several localities.*

1166. When bright red specks resembling spattered blood appear on linen, it is held to be a token of misfortune, probably of death. *Northern Ohio.*

1167. If the candle burns blue, it is token of a death.

1168. To see a coffin in the candle is a token of death. *Boston, Mass.*

1169. To see a "winding-sheet" in the candle has the same significance. *Virginia.*

1170. Three lamps or candles burned close together mean death.
Virginia.

1171. If a sudden and unaccountable light is seen in a carpenter's shop, it indicates that the carpenter will soon have to make a coffin.
Cape Breton.

1172. If a coffin creaks in a carpenter's shop, another order soon follows. *Newark, N. J., and Virginia.*

1173. If the coffin does not settle down smoothly into place in the grave, but has to be raised and lowered again, another in the family will die inside a year. *Stevens Point, Wis.*

1174. Change a sick person from one room to another, and he will die. *New Jersey.*

1175. If a clock, long motionless, suddenly begins to tick or strike, it is a sign of approaching death or misfortune.
Newark, N. J., Virginia, and North Carolina.

1176. If a corpse remains soft and supple after death, another death in the family will follow.
Trinity Bay, N. F., and Prince Edward Island.

1177. A cow mooing after midnight means death.

1178. To dance on the ground indicates disaster, or death within a year. *Boxford, Mass.*

1179. The hearing, in the wall, of the "death-watch," or "death-tick," betokens a death in the house.
General in the United States.

1180. A dish-cloth hung on a door-knob is a sign of death in a family. *Deerfield, Mass.*

1181. To knock on a door and receive no answer is a sign of death. *Virginia and Englewood, Ill.*

1182. The last name a dying person calls is that of the next to follow. *New Hampshire.*

1183. Sometimes the dying call for an absent one, as if in trouble. This is a sign that that person will have some great trouble in after life. *New York.*

1184. Death takes place at ebb tide. *New England Coast.*

1185. The person on whom the eyes of a dying person last rest will be the first to die. *Boston, Mass.*

~~1186.~~ It is a sign of death to see a flower blossoming out of season, as, for example, a rose in the fall.) This has proved a true omen in several cases, according to the experience of a lady who believes in these signs. In consequence of this belief, when she has such a a flower, she will pick it off the stem and throw it away, without mentioning the incident to any one. *Niagara Falls, Ont.*

1187. It is a sign of death to see a tree blossoming in the fall.
Orange Co., Va.

1188. If a garment is cut out on Friday, the person for whom it is made will not live unless it is finished on the same day.
Southern Indiana.

1189. If you begin a quilt on Friday, you will never live to finish it. *Maine.*

An act of this sort gave great distress to a domestic servant, who, until after the completion of the quilt, daily expected disaster. This woman came from French Canada.

1190. If a doctor is called on Friday, the patient will surely die.
Cambridge, Mass.

1191. If a hearse is drawn by two white horses, death in the neighborhood will occur within a month. *Central Maine.*

1192. If any one comes to a funeral after the procession starts, another death will occur in the same house. *Ohio.*

1193. At a funeral the first person who turns away from the grave will have the next death in his family. *Trinity Bay, N. F.*

1194. If one goes to a funeral with the intention of following to the grave but does not do so, a death soon follows in his family.
Virginia.

1195. If it rains during a burial, another member of the family will soon follow.
Poland, Me., Baldwinsville, N. Y., Ohio, and Alabama.

1196. If rain falls into an open grave, another burial in the same cemetery will occur within three days. *Western New York.*

1197. If you meet a funeral train, it is a sign of death.
Prince Edward Island.

1198. Do not let any one wear your hat to a funeral when you 've not worn it before yourself. *Massachusetts.*

1199. Whoever counts the carriages at a passing funeral will die within the year. *Peabody, Mass., and Hennepin, Ill.*
Or, some one will die.

1200. If shot remain in the gun after firing, some one of your family will die. *Labrador.*

1201. If you build on to your house, you will die within the year. *Labrador.*

1202. Lie down on a table and you will die before the year is out. *Mattawamkeag, Me.*

1203. To hold a lamp over a sleeping person causes death. *Massachusetts.*

1204. To break a looking-glass is a sign of death in the family before the year closes. *General in the United States.*

1205. To break a looking-glass is a sign of death, or of bad luck, or seven years. This is quite a general belief. Domestic servants, and particularly superstitious persons, are often thrown into a panic by accidents of this sort.
General in the United States and Canada.

1206. If three persons look into a mirror at the same time, one will die within the year. *Peabody, Mass., and New Hampshire.*

1207. If one try on mourning when not wearing it, he will have occasion to wear it soon. *Pennsylvania.*

1208. To put on a bonnet or hat of one in mourning is a sign that you will wear one before the year is out.
Peabody and Boston, Mass., and Niagara Falls, Ont.

1209. To drive a nail on Sunday is a sign that some one in the family will die within the year. *Pigeon Cove, Mass.*

1210. Hearing an imaginary rap and opening an outside door lets death in. *Ferrisburgh, Vt.*

1211. The hearing of three raps is a sign that some member of the family is dead. *Boston, Mass., and Orange Co., Va.*

1212. If members of a family, after long separation, meet for reunion, some one of the members will die within the year. *Cambridge, Mass.*

1213. Ringing in the ears is a sign of death. *General.*

1214. Ringing in the ears means death before the week ends. Of this ringing the term "death-bell" is used. It may be said by a country woman: "Oh! I have heard a death-bell!" or, "What a death-bell in my ear! You will hear of a death before the week is out." In case of a sudden death, such a person might say: "I am not surprised; I heard a death-bell on such a day."

Northern Ohio.

1215. The term "death-bell" is also a popular one in

Prince Edward Island.

1216. In some localities the direction of the apparent ringing indicates the direction from which the news of death will come.

1217. If an empty rocking-chair is seen to sway back and forth when apparently unoccupied, it is supposed that the chair is held by the spirit of some deceased member of the family, who has come back to choose the next to go, and call that person quickly.

Michigan.

1218. A spot resembling iron-rust on the finger means death.

Maine.

1219. Beginning on Saturday a garment that cannot be finished means death. *Ohio.*

1220. Deaths do not come singly; but if one of a family dies, a second death in the same family will occur within a year.

Cambridge, Mass.

1221. Whoever works on a sick person's dress, he or she will die within the year. *Massachusetts.*

1222. If some one is sick and a storm comes, it is a sign he will die during its continuance. *Virginia.*

1223. When a woman who has been sewing puts her thimble on the table as she sits down to eat, it is a sign that she will be left a widow if she marries. *Central Maine.*

1224. If one sings at a table while the family are eating, it means the death of a friend. *Webster City, Iowa.*

Or bad luck (*Virginia*); disappointment (*New Jersey*).

1225. If three drops of blood fall from your nose, one of your family is dead. *Labrador.*

1226. If you sneeze on Sunday morning before breakfast, you will hear of the death of some person you know before the next Saturday night.   *Northern Vermont.*

1227. If you sneeze at table with the mouth full, an acquaintance will die soon.   *Virginia and Alabama.*

1228. When sowing grain, if a strip of land is missed there will be a death inside of a year.   *Ohio and Maryland.*

1229. When you shiver, it means that some one is walking over the place where your grave is to be.
                    General in the United States.
1230. If sparks are left (unintentionally) in the ashes over night, it is a sign of death.   *Cumberland, Md.*

1231. If sparks of fire fly out of an opened stove door, it is a sign of death.   *Trinity Bay, N. F.*

1232. If any one in the town lies dead over Sunday, there will be another death before the end of the week.   *Bedford, Mass.*

1233. Three horses of the same color indicate death, but this sign is not very noticeable in a thickly settled community.
                    Baldwinsville, N. Y.
1234. Three chairs placed accidentally in a row mean death.
                    Ohio.
1235. If there is a death there will be three deaths in the family within a short time.   *New York.*

1236. To break the spell of thirteen at table, all should rise together, otherwise the first up (or, as some say, the last down) dies inside a twelvemonth.   *New England.*

1237. If thirteen sit at table, the one who rises first will not live through the year.
                    Somerville, Mass., Newark, N. J., and Mifflintown, Pa.
1238. If thirteen sit at table, the last one who sits down will not die that year.   *Brookline, Mass.*

1239. If window-shades fall down without being molested, it is a sign of death.   *Cape Breton.*

CHAPTER XVIII.

MORTUARY CUSTOMS.

1240. If "salt water pigeons'" feathers are in a bed, the sick person on it will not die easily. *Newfoundland.*

1241. In old colonial burying-grounds — in Plymouth, Concord, Cambridge, and Rutland, Mass. — the graves are so placed that the headstones face west, that is, the body lies with the feet toward the east. *Perhaps general in New England.*

1242. Among Irish Catholics it is usual to place the body with the feet toward the door. (The body of a young girl is usually draped in the robes of the society to which in her church she belonged. Over the corpse is constructed a white canopy, from one end of which images of white doves are often hung.) At the feet is a stand or table, on which flowers are laid, and where, at night, candles are kept burning. *Boston, Mass.*

1243. Country people turn the mirror to face the wall while one lies dead in the house. *Northern Ohio.*

1244. While the corpse is in the house, the looking-glass must be turned toward the wall; otherwise, whoever looks into the mirror will die within the year. This custom is said to be most common among Irish Catholics, but it is not confined to them.
Baldwinsville, N. Y.

1245. Bad luck (instead of death) is also said to follow violation of this rule. *Washington, D. C.*

1246. If, when any one dies, you put the coffin in any other room than the one the corpse is in, some other member of the family will die within a year. *Western Massachusetts.*

1247. "I have noticed at funerals of the aged, that when elderly people passed by the casket they would touch the forehead of the dead person. I was confident that there was some superstition connected with the act, because the same look was apparent on every face; but on being asked why this was done, they pretended it was bidding an old comrade good-bye. At last one told me that it was that they might not dream of the dead or see them."

Westport, Mass.

1248. It is usual, after the conclusion of the funeral service, for the persons present at the ceremony to pass in front of the dead, and look on the face. Not to perform this token of respect is felt as a lack of propriety. It is not uncommon for the undertaker, or some person in charge of the proceedings, to say in a loud voice: "An opportunity is now offered to those who desire to look on the face of the corpse," or words to that effect.

General in the United States.

1249. Only male relatives take part in the funeral procession.

Philadelphia, Pa.

1250. In regard to the ceremonies at the grave, usage differs widely. In New England it is usual for near relatives to attend; and, in the case of important persons, for a procession to march to the cemetery. Among Catholics a great number of friends attend the hearse of persons in humble life.

1251. It is an old Connecticut custom that the yard gate should never be shut after being opened to let through a body being carried from its former home to the graveyard.

1252. The funeral procession must not cross a river.

Baldwinsville, N. Y.

1253. "I was first led to notice the superstition about crossing a river, from having to attend funerals on the south side, when they would otherwise have been held on the north side. This is losing ground, owing to the frequency of crossing to reach the cemetery, but I had an instance only last spring." *Baldwinsville, N. Y.*

1254. The corpse must not pass twice over any part of the same road. *Baldwinsville, N. Y.*

1255. It is unlucky in a funeral, for those present to repass the house where death has occurred. *Baldwinsville, N. Y.*

1256. At a funeral, entering church before the mourners means death to some of the entering party. *Boston, Mass.*

1257. It is a bad sign to drive past a funeral procession.

Maine.

1258. It is unlucky to pass through a funeral procession, either between the carriages or the files of mourners on foot.

This is a general superstition. The custom, which has become instinctive with many persons, is usually set down to the score of decency and propriety. *General in the United States.*

1259. To meet a funeral is bad luck. To avert it, turn round and take three steps backward before going on. *St. John, N. B.*

1260. It is bad luck to meet a corpse. One may follow it, but never meet it.) A colored person will turn square about on seeing a funeral procession approaching. *Talladega, Ala., and Virginia.*

1261. To keep the corpse in the house over Sunday will bring death in the family before the year is out.
South Framingham, Mass.
1262. If the grave is left open over Sunday, another death will occur before the Sunday following. *Boxford, Mass.*

1263. If a grave is covered on Friday, another in the same family will follow inside of a year. *Chatham, N. B.*

1264. If a grave is left open over night without the corpse, another death in the family will soon follow. *Virginia.*

1265. It is bad to disturb an old grave, as by putting up a tombstone ; you will thus herald a death. *Chestertown, Md.*

1266. Many will not go through a graveyard on the way to call on friends, for fear of bringing death into the house.
Massachusetts.
1267. The clothes of the dead wear out quickly.
Westport, Mass.
1268. "The clothes of the dead never wear long" when used by the living. *New York.*

1269. If you put clothes of a live person on a corpse, when the clothes decay the owner will die. *St. Joseph, Mo.*

1270. It is quite customary, both in the United States and in Canada, to give the whole house a thorough cleaning after a death has occurred, even when the deceased has undergone no prolonged illness and has died of no contagious disease. A day or two after the funeral one sometimes sees, particularly in country homes, feather beds, mattresses, etc., etc., put out to air. Sometimes even rooms are whitewashed in the purification process.

CHAPTER XIX.

MISCELLANEOUS.

ACTIONS.

1271. IF a child in eating an apple merely girdles it and leaves the apple good at stem and below, it indicates that he will be a poor man ; the saying is, "a poor man's core."

1272. It is unlucky to turn back after starting to go anywhere. To avert misfortune after turning back, make the sign of the cross in the dust with the heel, and spit in the cross.
Arkansas (negro), and Kentucky.

1273. It is unlucky to turn back after having once started out.
Quebec.

1274. To get out of bed on the wrong side puts one out all day. "He got out of bed with the wrong foot foremost" is said of a person who has a fit of crossness. *Northern Ohio.*

1275. To drop your books on the way to school signifies that you will make mistakes in your lessons. *Chestertown, Md.*

1276. Drop a book and you will miss your lesson, unless it is immediately picked up and kissed. *Alabama.*

1277. Whoever eats the last piece of bread will be an old maid.
Pennsylvania.

1278. If you break something, you will break two other things.
Maine, Massachusetts, and Northern Ohio.

1279. To twirl a chair on one leg means that you are going to fight with somebody. *Peabody, Mass.*

1280. Whirling an empty chair indicates that a whipping is in store for the transgressor.

1281. If you twirl a chair around on one leg, it is a sign that you are about to break dishes. *Chestertown, Md.*

1282. You must n't pay the doctor entirely, or there will be sickness in the family. *Lonsdale, R. I.*

1283. You must leave by the door through which you enter there will be trouble with the family, or ill luck to yourself.
Pennsylvania.

1284. If you leave by any other door than the one through which you have entered, it is said that you will not come again.
Cumberland, Me.

1285. In bathing, the eyes should always be rubbed towards the nose, as that makes them large, and rubbing out the opposite way makes them small.
Cambridge, Mass.

1286. In climbing a fence, —

> Get over, meet with clover,
> Get through, meet with a shoe ;
> Get under, meet with a blunder.
Sunderland, Mass.

1287. If you step on a grave, you will never grow any more.
Chestertown, Md. (negro).

1288. Step over a living thing, and that thing, whether a human being or not, will not grow any more.
Province of Quebec, Can.

1289. To step over one leg of a child will cause it to grow longer than the other.
Baltimore, Md.

1290. To comb the hair after dark is a sign of sickness.

> Comb your hair after dark,
> Comb sorrow to your heart.
Connecticut.

1291. If you comb your hair after dark, it will make you forgetful.
Northern Ohio.

1292. If the right hand itches, you are going to get money ; if the left, you will shake hands with a friend.   If the nose itches, a friend is coming.
Talladega, Ala.

1293. Two persons wiping hands on the same towel and twisting it occasions a quarrel.
Pennsylvania.

1294. Wash and wipe together,
> Live in peace together.
Northern Ohio.

1295. If two persons wash their hands at the same time, it is a sign that they will be friends forever.
Alabama.

1296. If two persons wipe their hands at the same time, they will be foes forever.
Alabama.

1297. When two persons put one hand of each flat together, palm to palm, they will quarrel. *Province of Quebec, Can.*

1298. If two persons clasp hands so as to lock the fingers, bringing the palm of one person against the palm of the other person's hand, it will break friendship. *Newton, Mass.*

1299. If you hug your knee (hold your knee in clasped hands), you will hug up trouble. *Salem and Medford, Mass.*

1300. When your joints crack, it is a sign that you have not outlived your best days. *New York, N. Y.*

1301. If you kiss through a veil, there 'll be a coolness.
Portland, Me.

1302. Crossed knives are a sign of a quarrel.
Cumberland, Mass.

1303. Stir with a knife,
Stir up strife.

1304. Never look after a friend who is leaving you till he is quite out of sight, or you will never see him or her again ; but turn your eyes away while he is still visible, that he or she may return.
General in the United States.

1305. Never say " good-by " more than once. *Alabama.*

1306. One who habitually bites the nails is ill-natured.
Ohio.

1307. If you bite your finger-nails you will always be poor.
Massachusetts.

1308. If you sleep with your head towards the north, it will prevent sickness. *General in the United States.*

1309. If you can cut a pie fair and true, you 'll have a likely husband. If you make the slices uneven, he 'll be crooked.

1310. If you make a bed handsomely, you 'll have a handsome husband.

1311. If you cut pie straight, you will go to housekeeping.
If you cut pie crooked, you will have no house to keep.
New Hampshire.

1312. If you make a rhyme involuntarily, you will have a present.
New Brunswick.

1313. The free use of salt is a sign of having a temper.
Lynn, Mass.

1314. To say anything backward is a sign you will get a present.
Peabody, Mass.

1315. If you sing before you eat,
You 'll cry before you sleep.
Ohio and Iowa.

1316. If you sing before breakfast, you will cry before supper.
Cambridge, Mass.

1317. If you laugh before breakfast, you will cry before supper.
Prince Edward Island and Somerville, Mass.

1318. Little birds that sing in the morning
The old cat will catch before night.

Accustomed to be said to children when they were especially hilarious in the early morning. *Northern Ohio.*

1319. If a child sing before breakfast, it will get a whipping before night. *New Hampshire.*

1320. To sing after you go to bed is a sign that tears will come before breakfast. *Maine.*

1321. If the sole of either foot itches, you will walk on strange ground. *Boston, Mass.*

1322. When about to begin a new enterprise, one must not step over straws in starting out.

1323. If you stumble with the right foot, it means a glad surprise.
Pennsylvania (negro).

1324. In going anywhere, if you strike the right foot you will be welcome wherever you may be going, and if the same happens to the left foot, you will be on strange ground. *Bellville, O.*

1325. To sit on a table is a sign of coming disappointment.
Maine and Massachusetts.

1326. In drinking tea, if you take a stem in the mouth it means an enemy ; you must bite it and throw it over the right shoulder.
Central Maine.

1327. If you stub your toe going into a house, you are not wanted there. *Guilford, Conn.*

1328. If, in going visiting, you stub the right toe, you are welcome ; if the left, you are unwelcome. *Massachusetts and Ohio.*

1329. If you stub your toe going anywhere, it means a disappointment.   *Bathurst, N. B.*

1330. Stub your toe,
   Lose your beau.
                                              Salem, Mass.

1331. To bite the tongue while talking means that you have told a lie.

1332. If you bite your tongue suddenly while eating, it is a sign some one is coming hungry.   *Cambridge, Mass.*

1333. In going along the street or path, where there is a tree, go inside rather than outside the tree, for you will be disappointed if you take the latter course.   *Eastern Massachusetts.*

1334. In drinking water, if you glance over the glass, you are a flirt.   *Pennsylvania.*

1335. Whistling girls and crowing hens
   Always come to some bad ends.
                                              General in the United States.

1336. Whistling girls and sheep
   Are the very worst cattle a farmer can keep.

1337. A whistling girl and a laughing sheep,
   Are the very best property a man can keep.
                                              Northern Ohio.

1338. Girls that whistle and hens that crow
   Make their way wherever they go.

1339. Whistle before you eat,
   Cry before you sleep.
                                              Baldwinsville, N. Y.

BODILY AFFECTIONS.

1340. If the right cheek burns, some one is speaking well of you ; if the left, they are speaking ill of you ; if both, they speak well and ill at once.   Moisten the finger in the mouth and touch it to the cheek, naming those whom you suspect ; the one at whose name it grows cool was speaking of you.   *New Brunswick.*

1341. If your right ear burns, some one is talking well of you ; if your left, he is talking ill.   *General in the United States.*

1342. If you bite the corner of your apron, you will make back-biters bite their tongues. *Pennsylvania.*

1343. Pinch your ear, and the person talking of you will bite his own tongue.

1344. If the right ear burns, it is a sign that some one is thinking well of you; if the left ear burns, it is a sign that some one is thinking unkindly of you; but if both ears burn, friend and foe are fighting about you. *Pennsylvania.*

1345. If your ears burn, people are talking well of you; if your ears are cold, the contrary. *New Hampshire.*

1346. If your right ear burns, a lady is speaking of you; if the left, a man. *Maine and Pennsylvania.*

1347. If your left ear itches, some one is saying unpleasant things about you; but if your right ear, pleasant things. Some say, —
> Both left and right
> Are good at night.
>
> *Cambridge, Mass.*

1348. If the right eye itches, it is a sign you will cry; if the left, you will laugh, because R stands for "roar" and L for "laugh." *Baldwinsville, N. Y.*

1349. If the right eye itches, you'll laugh; if the left eye, you'll cry. *Boston, Mass.*

1350. If your eye itches, some one wants to see you and can't. *Peabody, Mass.*

1351. If you look at one who has inflamed eyes, you'll catch the disease. *Maine and Ohio.*

1352. If your elbow itches, you will sleep with a stranger. *Boston, Mass.*

1353. If the right foot itches, it is a sign you will go where you will be welcome; if the left foot itches, it is a sign you will go where you are unwelcome. *Baldwinsville, N. Y.*

1354. If while going to see any one your left foot itches, you are not welcome. *Alabama.*

1355. The nose itching is a sign you are going to "get mad." *Peabody, Mass.*

1356. If your nose itches, it is a sign of a present.

1357. If your nose itches, some one will be provoked with you.

1358. If your nose itches, it is a sign that

> You 'll be mad,
> See a stranger,
> Kiss a fool,
> Or be in danger.
>
> *Prince Edward Island.*

1359. If your nose itches, you will

> See a stranger,
> Kiss a fool,
> Or be in danger.
>
> *Peabody, Mass.*

1360. If your nose itches, it is a sign you will be kissed, cussed, or vexed. *Somerville, Mass.*

1361. If the nose itches, some say you will receive a letter ; others declare it is a sign your lover is thinking of you.
Baldwinsville, N. Y.

1362. If the palm of the hand itches, it is a good sign that you will kill something. *Labrador.*

1363. Itching in the palm is a sign of a fight, or of seeing a stranger.

1364. An unexpected scratch denotes surprise.

1365. A long scratch across the palm denotes a sleigh-ride.
Pennsylvania (negro).

1366. A scratch on the hand denotes a ride ; the length of the scratch indicates the length of the ride. *New England.*

1367. A scratch on the right hand is a sign of a ride to come ; on the left, a disappointment. *Baldwinsville, N. Y.*

1368. If your knee itches, you are jealous. *Boston, Mass.*

1369. Being lousy is an indication that the lousy person is in good health. *Newfoundland.*

1370. Some hold that the white spots that one has on the fing
nails represent the lies you have told.

Maine and Baldwinsville, N. Y.

1371. If you shudder without apparent cause, some one has
stepped over or upon your grave. *Gilsum, N. H.*

1372. If you shudder, it is a sign that a rabbit is running across,
or a goose is eating grass from your grave. *Chestertown, Md.*

1373. There is an old superstition that every sigh causes a drop of
blood to flaw from the heart. *Exeter, N. H.*

1374. "Smooches" made on the face by soiled fingers (called
beauty spots in Ohio) mean a present. *New Brunswick.*

1375. A lump on the tongue means that you have told a lie.
Prince Edward Island, New York, and Northern Ohio.

APPAREL.

1376. If you mend your apron or dress while on you, some one
will lie about you. *Maine and Alabama.*

1377. As many stitches as you take (in mending a garment while
wearing it), so many lies will be told about you.

New Hampshire.

1378. If a garment is mended while being worn, it is a sign the
wearer will do something he is ashamed of before the week is out.

Newton, Mass.

1379. If one mends his clothes upon his back,
It is a sign his trouble will never come back.

Connecticut.

1380. Basting threads left in a garment signify that it is not yet
paid for. *Massachusetts and Ohio.*

1381. Put your clothes on the wrong side out and you'll have a
present before the week is out. *Peabody, Mass.*

1382. If, when dressing, one puts on any of his clothing wrong
side out, it is a sign that he will soon receive a present.

Alabama.

1383. If you happen to put your skirt on wrong side out, you are
likely to get a new one. *Alabama.*

1384. You must n't talk when some article of dress you are wearing is being mended, or some one will talk or tell lies about you.

1385. In dressing for a journey, if you wish to have good luck, dress the right foot first.   *Belleville, Ohio.*

1386. If the hem of a lady's dress turns up, she is sure to have a new one.   *Alabama.*

1387. While sewing on a garment, should you sew it to your dress by mistake, as many stitches as you take, so many lies will be told about you.   *Baldwinsville, N. Y.*

1388. If you break your needle in making a dress, you will live to wear it out. If you tear a hole in a new dress, the first time wearing it, you will have a new one before that is worn out.
                    Deer Isle, Me.
1389. If you break a needle in sewing a new gown, it is a sure sign you will live to wear out the garment.   *Holyoke, Mass.*

1390. If you break your needle in making a garment, or have to rip out some of it, you will live to wear it out.   *Boston, Mass.*

1391. If a white petticoat falls below your dress, it is a sign that your father loves you better than your mother.   *New England.*

1392. Crooked pins are a sign that the owner is an old maid.
                    Province of Quebec, Can.
1393. Should a friend withdraw a ring from the finger of another, it is a sign it will break friendship. The owner should take off the ring and hand it to the friend.   *Baldwinsville, N. Y.*

1394. A hole in the toe of your shoe or stocking, so as to show the toe, means a letter.   *Cape Breton.*

1395. Old shoes, particularly the soles, were often buried by negro servants on Monday morning to keep the devil down through the week.   *Chestertown, Md.*

1396. Save the old shoes to throw after the carriage, when any of the family start on a journey ; it will insure a safe return.
                    Massachusetts.

1397. Wear the boot (or shoe) on the side, a rich man's bride;
On the toe, spend as you go;
On the heel, love to do weel;
On the ball, live to spend all.
Boston.

1398. Hole in the toe, spend as you go:
Hole at the side, be a rich bride;
Hole at the heel, spend as you feel;
Hole on the ball, live to spend all.
New York.

1399. Wear at the toe, live to see woe;
Wear at the side, live to be a bride;
Wear at the ball, live to spend all;
Wear at the heel, live to save a deal.
New York.

1400. Wear on the toe,
Spend as you go;
Wear on the ball,
Love to spend all.
Wear on the side,
You 'll be a rich bride.

1401. Of stockings :—
Wear at the toe,
Spend as you go:
Wear at the heel,
Spend a good deal;
Wear at the ball,
You 'll live to spend all.
South Carolina.

CUSTOMS.

1402. Halloween cabbages are pulled and thrown against the owner's door as a reminder of his laziness.
Southern Pennsylvania and Ohio.

1403. Shelled corn is thrown at every one — the significance not known.
Southern Pennsylvania.

1404. If a man is insulted and means to be revenged, he will bare his arm and cut a cross in it with his knife, called a " vengeance mark."
Mountains of North Carolina.

1405. If you wash your face in dew before sunrise on May Day, you will become very beautiful.
Alabama.

1406. Dry spots, where there is no dew, are called "fairy rings."
Salem, Mass.

1407. Run round a fairy ring twice on Easter Sunday morning, and fairies will arise and follow you. *Salem, Mass.*

1408. The looking-glass is often turned with the face to the wall, or taken out of the room during a thunder-storm, because "quicksilver is so bad to draw the lightning." *Bathurst, N. B.*

1409. You are said to "take the manners" if you take the last of any kind of food from a plate. *New England.*

1410. "Manners dish" is the dish put on for show, and not expected to be eaten. *Northern Ohio.*

1411. Homœopathic pills must be taken in odd numbers.
New England.

1412. When a meteor is seen, Catholics often say, "A soul is ascending into heaven."

1413. A present of a knife or any pointed instrument cuts friendship ; always sell it for a penny.

1414. A present of pins breaks friendship.
General in the United States.

1415. There was a superstition among old people who had never been much abroad, in the town where I was born (Stratham, N. H.), that if they were photographed they were likely to die soon after, and many rather objected on that account.
Stratham, N. H.

1416. After sneezing, it is customary to say, "God bless you."
General in the United States.

1417. A bit of steel, such as a needle, protects one from witches.
Brookline, Mass.

1418. A thief may be detected by a key turning in the Bible to Psalm i. 18–21, when the name of the guilty person is mentioned.
Labrador.

DAYS.

1419. What you do on your birthday, you will do all the year.
Salem, Mass.

1420. On cutting the finger-nails : —
Cut them on Monday, cut them for news,
Cut them on Tuesday, a pair of new shoes,

Cut them on Wednesday, cut them for health,
Cut them on Thursday, cut them for wealth,
Cut them on Friday, cut them for sorrow,
Cut them on Saturday, see your sweetheart to-morrow,
Cut them on Sunday, cut them for evil,
All the whole week you 'll be ruled by the devil.

Baldwinsville, N. Y.

1421. If you wear a garment for the first time on Saturday, you
will have another one before it is worn out. *Bedford, Mass.*

1422. Study on Sunday, forget it through the week.

Nashua, N. H.

1423. If, of your own accord, you leave home for Sunday visiting,
you will be forced to leave for two Sundays following.

Labrador.

1424. Get a letter on Monday, and you 'll get six during that
week. *New York, N. Y.*

1425. If you break anything on Monday, you will break something every day in the week. *Somerville, Mass.*

1426. If you break anything Sunday, you will continue to do so
every day of the week, or as you commence Sunday, so you will go
through the week. *Eastern Massachusetts.*

1427. If you begin anything Saturday, it must be finished that
day or it will not get finished. *Boston, Mass.*

1428. Sneeze on Monday, sneeze for a letter,
Sneeze on Tuesday, sneeze for something better,
Sneeze on Wednesday, sneeze for news,
Sneeze on Thursday, sneeze for a new pair of shoes,
Sneeze on Friday, sneeze for sorrow,
Sneeze on Saturday, see him to-morrow.

Niagara Falls, Ont.

1429. Sneeze on Monday, sneeze for danger,
Sneeze on Tuesday, kiss a stranger,
Sneeze on Wednesday, receive a letter,
Sneeze on Thursday, something better,
Sneeze on Friday, sneeze for sorrow,
Sneeze on Saturday, see your true love to-morrow.
Sneeze on Sunday, your safety seek,
Or the devil will have you the rest of the week.

Crown Point, N. Y.

1430. Sneeze before twelve and one, and you will hear news.
Brighton, Mass.

1431. Sneeze at the table, there will be one more or one less at the next meal. *Alabama.*

1432. Sneeze before your breakfast,
See your beau before the day is past.
Brighton, Mass.

1433. If you sneeze once, a girl is thinking of you ; twice, she is wishing for you ; thrice, it is a sign of a cold. *Alabama.*

1434. Sneeze before seven,
Sneeze before eleven.
Boston, Mass.

1435. What you sew on Sunday, you 'll take out on Monday.
What you sew on Sunday, you 'll rip out in heaven.
Massachusetts.

1436. Never cut your toe-nails Sunday, or you will do something to be ashamed of before the week is out. *Granville, Mass.*

1437. Cut your nails Monday morning, without speaking (?), and you will get a present before the week is out ; some have it, "without thinking of a red fox's tail," instead of "without speaking."
Westport, Mass.

DOMESTIC LIFE.

1438. It is supposed that a broom placed behind the door will keep off witches. *Bruynswick, N. Y.*

1439. To burn the stub of a broom or break a sugar-bowl, means a quarrel. *Westport, Mass.*

1440. A spark seen on a candle or lamp when the light is extinguished means the receipt of a letter.
St. John, N. B., and Salem, Mass.

1441. Wet the finger and touch the "letter" on the candle. If it come off on the finger, it means a letter for you. *Maine.*

1442. The letter in the candle will face the one for whom the letter is to be. If the little snuff bud is bright, it means a letter.
Northern Ohio.

1443. If the candle is sooty, or shows a spark in the wick on blowing out, it is a sign that a letter is on its way.

1444. If chairs become entangled (legs interlaced, etc.), it means a quarrel. *Bathurst, N. B.*

1445. If you choke (food gets in the windpipe), it means some one has told lies about you. *Cape Breton.*

1446. It is a sign of good old-fashioned economy to use up a dish-cloth until it can be put into your mouth. *Massachusetts.*

1447. If a door opens of itself, it is supposed to indicate the presence of a spirit, usually one of the family. *Massachusetts.*

1448. It is unlucky to name a child after a dead child of the family. *Newfoundland.*

1449. If you begin keeping house with many in the family, it is a sign that you will always have a large family or houseful.
Ohio.

1450. If a wood fire snaps and sparkles, each time it does indicates the receipt of a letter. *Peabody, Mass.*

1451. One of the negro superstitions was that when the fire burned with a blue flame, it was the devil seeking to speak to them. A handful of salt would make him go away. *Alabama.*

1452. Sweep the floor after dark, you 'll see sickness before morning.

1453. If while eating you drop food on the floor, it is a sign that some one is telling lies about you. *Cape Breton.*

1454. Food dropped on the floor by one signifies that some one grudges you it. *Common in the United States.*

1455. Do not change your place at table ; it is very unlucky.
New York, N. Y.

1456. If you keep changing your furniture to different places, you 'll be poor. *Massachusetts.*

1457. Not drinking the whole contents of a glass or cup means disappointment. *Westport, Mass.*

1458. If sooty bubbles form and blacken on the wick in a lamp burning whale oil, each bubble indicates the receipt of a letter.
Peabody, Mass.

1459. When sparks are seen on the bottom of the tea-kettle, it is a sign that folks are going home from meeting.
New Hampshire and Boxford, Mass.

1460. Sparks flying from a fire mean letters; the number of the sparks is the number of the letters. *Boston, Mass.*

1461. If a spark or sparks jump out of the fire and hit you or come towards you, it is a sign some one has a spite or grudge against you. *Bathurst, N. B.*

1462. Two spoons given to one person denotes that that person will have two homes before the year is out. *Chestertown, Md.*

1463. The tea-kettle suddenly singing means news.
Patten, Me.

VARIOUS.

1464. A stratum of warm air indicates the presence of the devil.
Boston, Mass. (Irish).

1465. If, when a newly-married couple go to housekeeping, she slyly takes her mother's dish-cloth or dish-wiper, she will never be homesick. Old Mrs. —— told me that she believed that was the reason she was not homesick when they moved from Pennsylvania to Ohio. *Ohio.*

1466. To have a sharp knife is a sign of a lazy man.
Central Maine.

1467. Passing anything through a ladder is a sign of a long passage. *Conception Bay, N. F.*

1468. If a ship has a starboard list, it is a sign of a quick passage; if a port list, it is a sign of a long passage.
Conception Bay and New Harbor, N. F.

1469. Write the date of the first snowstorm, and you'll gain a bet before the winter is through. *Massachusetts.*

1470. To ascertain a girl's age, pull a hair from her head, hang a finger-ring from this inside a tumbler or goblet, and it will strike the number of years. *Boston, Mass.*

1471. Throw a strand of your hair in the fire; if it blazes you will live long and happily; if not, you will die soon. *Alabama.*

1472. If a tree falls to the right while you are looking at it, you are going on a long trip before the end of the year, and will have some unexpected piece of good luck. *Alabama.*

1473. A person born on Halloween is said to be possessed of evil spirits. *Alabama.*

1474. Place a broom across the door, and if any of your departed friends wish to speak to you they are free to come and go at will while the broom remains there. *Alabama.*

1475. If a person who raises fowls is bothered with hawks, he may prevent the trouble by throwing a handful of " rocks " into the fire while it is burning brightly. *Alabama.*

NOTES.

NOTES.

INTRODUCTION, PAGE 8. — S. G. Drake, *Annals of Witchcraft in New England*, Boston, 1869, p. 189, remarks that the principal accusers and witnesses in the witchcraft prosecutions of 1692, in Salem, Mass., were eight girls from eleven to twenty years of age, and adds with reference to their conduct previous to the accusations : " These Females instituted frequent Meetings, or got up, as it would now be styled, a Club, which was called a Circle. How frequent they had these Meetings is not stated, but it was soon ascertained that they met to 'try projects,' or to do or produce superhuman Acts. They doubtless had among them some book or books on Magic, and Stories of Witchcraft, which one or more of their Circle professed to understand, and pretended to teach the Rest." An examination of the evidence in the trials, however, shows not only no authority for these assertions, but that no such meetings took place previous to the trials, nor did any such "circle" exist. Drake derived his information from a paper by S. P. Fowler, who, in an address before the Essex Institute, in the year 1856, had remarked : "These girls, together with Abigail Williams, a niece of Mr. Parris, aged eleven years, were in the habit of meeting in a circle in the village, to practise palmistry, fortune-telling, &c." For such representation Mr. Fowler had no warrant ; it would seem that he had obtained the notion by transferring to the time of the trials his experience in connection with spiritualistic "circles" of his own day. It is curious to observe how readily this suggestion was adopted, and with what uniformity recent popular narratives of the delusion reiterate, with increasing positiveness of phrase, the unfounded assumption. The expression, to "try projects," is therefore taken by Mr. Drake from modern folk-lore. Fowler's address, entitled " An Account of the Life and Character of the Rev. Samuel Parris, of Salem Village, and of his Connection with the Witchcraft Delusion of 1692," was printed in the *Proceedings* of the Essex Institute, Salem, Mass., 1862, vol. ii. pp. 49–68 and also separately (Salem, 1857). For assistance in determining the origin of Drake's statement I am indebted to Mr. Abner C. Goodell, Jr., of Salem, Mass. — *W. W. N.*

Nos. 15–16. — The reader who is interested to know how much importance has been attributed to the caul will do well to consult Levinus Lemnius, *De Miraculis Occultis Naturæ.* Chapter viii. of Book II. is headed : De infantium recens natorum galeis, seu tenui mollique membrana, qua facies tanquam larva, aut personata tegmine obducta, ad primum lucis intuitum se spectandam exhibet.

The belief in the efficacy of the caul goes back at least to the time of St. Chrysostom, who, in the latter part of the fourth century, preached against this with kindred superstitions. Advertisements of cauls for sale, at prices ranging from twenty guineas down, have from time to time appeared in the London papers as recently as the middle of the present century, if not even later.

No. 60. — See "Current Superstitions," *Journal of American Folk-Lore*, vol. ii. No. V.

Nos. 116–118. — The custom of consulting in augury the occasional white spots on the finger-nails still survives, despite the protestation of old Sir Thomas Browne. He says : —

" That temperamental dignotions, and conjecture of prevalent humours, may be collected from spots in our Nails, we are not averse to concede. But yet not ready to admit sundry divinations vulgarly raised upon them. Nor do we observe it verified in others, what *Cardan* discovered as a property in himself : to have found therein signs of most events that ever happened unto him. Or that there is much considerable in that doctrine of Cheiromancy, that spots in the top of the Nails do signifie things past ; in the middle, things present ; and at the bottom, events to come. That White specks presage our felicity ; Blue ones our misfortunes. That those in the Nail of the Thumb have significations of honour, those in the fore-Finger, of riches, and so respectively in other Fingers (according to Planetical relations, from whence they receive their names), as *Tricassus* hath taken up, and *Picciolus* well rejecteth."

No. 148. — A very complete account of the signification of moles is quoted from "The Greenwich Fortune Teller," in Brand's *Popular Antiquities* (Bohn's ed.), iii. 254.

CHAPTERS IV. AND V. — Two of the most interesting and most accessible lists of projects and Halloween observances are Gay's well-known *Shepherd's Week* and Burns's *Halloween*.

No. 170. — It is an interesting psychological fact that projects are in the great majority of cases tried by girls and young women rather than by boys and young men.

No. 174. — Here, as in many other cases, it is assumed that young men and women are accustomed to indulge in promiscuous kissing. The use of the word gentleman sufficiently indicates the level of society from which this project was obtained. Gentleman in this sense signifies any male human being over sixteen. It is often used more specifically to mean sweetheart, as " Mary and her gentleman were at the policemen's ball."

No. 184. — On Biblical divination see Brand's *Popular Antiquities* (Bohn's ed.), iii. 337, 338.

No. 186. — This custom of divining the color of the hair of one's future wife or husband, which is probably very old, yet survives in many places, but with interesting modifications as to the bird which gives the signal to try the divination. In Westphalia it is at sight of the first swallow that the peasant looks to see if there be a hair under his foot. According to Gay, in England it is the cuckoo.

> "When first the year I heard the cuckoo sing,
> And call with welcome note the budding spring,
> I straightway set a running with such haste
> Deborah that won the smock scarce ran so fast;
> Till spent for lack of breath, quite weary grown,
> Upon a rising bank I sat adown,
> There doffed my shoe; and by my troth I swear,
> Therein I spied this yellow frizzled hair,
> As like to Lubberkin's in curl and hue
> As if upon his comely pate it grew."

Nos. 187–193. — These practices, and others like No. 453 and the asseverations, Nos. 60–67, shade off insensibly into children's games, customs, and sayings. Games pure and simple have been omitted from the present monograph, since they are evidently out of place among superstitions. They have been admirably treated in Mr. Newell's *Games and Songs of American Children.* The customs and sayings for the most part belong in collections like Halliwell's *Nursery Rhymes* rather than in the present collection.

No. 211. — Projects in which flowers and leaves are employed certainly much antedate the Christian era. Theocritus (Idyll III.) describes one in which a poppy petal is used, and he also refers to another form of love-divination by aid of the leaf of the plant Telephilon.

No. 245. — It is probable that the direction in which one is to walk during the performance of this and similar acts of divination is not a matter of indifference, even when no direction is prescribed. One would expect to find it done sunwise. See note on Chapter xvi.

Nos. 254–256. — The *Sedum* has long enjoyed a reputation for aphrodisiac qualities, as is set forth in Gerarde's *Herbal* and other authorities. Perhaps the choice of the plant for use in this form of project is due to some lingering tradition of its potency, or it may be simply because of its great vitality and power of growing under adverse conditions.

No. 334. — I happen to know that in 1895 one bride, in a Boston suburb, wore seven yellow garters, at the request of seven girl friends. Probably the fashion of wearing yellow garters owes its present currency to the repute in which they are held as love-amulets.

Chapter VIII. — Some notion of the prevalence of a popular belief in the omens to be derived from dreams may be obtained from the fact that dream books are still enough in demand to warrant their publication. I have seen but one such volume. That was more than thirty years ago. A dream book is now published by a New York firm, and I find, from inquiries in Boston, that it sells at a moderate rate.

No. 626. — See Shoe Omens in Brand's *Popular Antiquities* (Bohn's ed.), iii. 166.

Nos. 785–789. — The curious reader will find an excellent summary of the beliefs in regard to sneezing in Brand's *Popular Antiquities*, vol. iii.

Nos. 796–800. — In New Hampshire it was formerly usual for young people to purchase gold beads, one at a time, with their earnings. When a sufficient number of beads was obtained the necklace was made, and after it had once been put on was never taken off by night or day. It is difficult to induce the elderly people who still retain these necklaces to part with them, there being a superstitious feeling in regard to the consequences.

Nos. 831, 832. — These cures and a few other superstitions have been taken from a very interesting paper, " Notes on the Folk-Lore of Newfoundland," in the *Journal of American Folk-Lore*, vol. viii. No. XXXI. Almost all of the other folk-lore from Newfoundland and Labrador has been given me by Rev. A. C. Waghorne. It is interesting to notice how among these seafaring people weather-lore predominates over all other kinds.

Nos. 845–848. — These devices for suppressing hiccoughs are scarcely superstitions in reality, as they doubtless often do relieve the nervous, spasmodic action of the respiratory muscles, by fixing the attention upon the cure. But in the popular mind some charm, I take it, is attributed to the counting, repeating, or what not.

CHAPTER XIII. — Several remedies for warts are here introduced which belong with the collection of animal and plant lore for which the writer has much material accumulated. In general such topics, including a very large number of saliva charms and cures, have been omitted from the present list.

Nos. 872, 880–882. — It is interesting to notice this illustration of the doctrine of signatures. Excrescences of such varied character, whether animal or vegetable, are supposed by contact to cause warts, doubtless simply because of the accidental resemblance.

Nos. 889–896. — It seems that any juices of peculiar or marked color are popularly credited with curative power. The plants whose juices are thought to cure warts are, it will be noticed, of wide botanical range. In all probability there is no similarity in the effects to be obtained from the application of their sap.

No. 979. — The somewhat unusual phenomenon of rain falling while the sun is shining seems to have so attracted the attention of the human mind as to have given rise to various sayings.

A native of Western Africa told me that among his tribe, the Vey people, it was always said when the sun shone as rain fell that it was a sign that a leopardess had just given birth to young.

In Japan the occurrence is said to indicate that a wedding procession of foxes is passing near by, and the children have a pretty habit of running to the supporting pillars of the house, to place the ear against the timbers and listen for the footfalls of the foxes. The little people also interlace their fingers in a certain way, then peeping through the chinks between the fingers they declare they can see the wedding train.

Nos. 1020–1028. — The mackerel sky is a name given to an assemblage of cirrus clouds which are thought to imitate the barred markings on the side of a mackerel. Mares' tails are wisp-like, curved cirri.

CHAPTER XV. — To illustrate the remarkable prevalence of a regard for the phases of the moon in the management of every-day affairs among the

Pennsylvania Germans, the following list of their beliefs is appended. All are from Buffalo Valley, Central Pennsylvania.[1]

THE MOON.

All cereals, when planted in the waxing of the moon, will germinate more rapidly than if planted in the waning of the moon.

The same is true of the ripening of grain.

Beans planted when the horns of the moon are up will readily pole, but if planted when the horns are down will not.

Plant early potatoes when the horns of the moon are up, else they will go too deep into the ground.

Plant late potatoes in the dark of the moon.

For abundance in anything, you must plant it when the moon is in the sign of the Twins.

Plant onions when the horns of the moon are down.

Pick apples in the dark of the moon, to keep them from rotting.

Make wine in the dark of the moon.

Make vinegar in the light of the moon.

Marry in the light of the moon.

Move in the light of the moon.

Butcher in the increase of the moon.

Boil soap in the increase of the moon.

Cut corn in the decrease of the moon, else it will spoil.

Spread manure when the horns of the moon are down.

Lay the first or lower rail of a fence when the horns of the moon are up. Put in the stakes and finish the fence when the horns are down.

Roof buildings when the horns of the moon are down, else the shingles will curl up at the edges and the nails will draw out.

Lay a board on the grass; if the horns of the moon are up, the grass will not be killed; if they are down, it will.

Cut your hair on the first Friday after the new moon.

Never cut your hair in the decrease of the moon.

Cut your corns in the decrease of the moon.

Nos. 1114–1123. — These superstitions regarding planting crops according to the moon are by no means idle sayings that have no influence over farmers. I know positively that in many parts of the United States and in Prince Edward Island gardens and fields are often planted after direct reference to the almanac in regard to the moon's changes. Metropolitan dwellers have small knowledge of what an important book the almanac is to many country people. In many a quiet farm home the appearance of the new almanac is looked forward to with great interest. Its arrival is welcomed, and it is hung up near the kitchen clock for constant reference. It is studied with care, especially on Sundays. The farmer or farm-wife, who would scorn to do an hour's work in the hay-field to save a crop from

___

[1] *Journal of American Folk-Lore*, vol. iv. No. XIII., " Folk-Lore from Buffalo Valley," J. H. Owens.

a Sunday shower, earnestly peruses the almanac to get rules to guide the week-day sowing and planting. There are old auguries, too, of whose import I am not definitely informed, to be derived from consulting the signs of the zodiac; auguries, I think, concerning human destiny as well as the planting of crops. Speaking of the place held by the almanac recalls one of those neighborhood anecdotes that by oft telling become classic. A young woman long ill, with consumption I believe, died very suddenly. Her brother, in speaking of the event, said : " Why, no, we never thought of Mary dying so soon. Why, she sat up in the big rocking-chair most all Sunday afternoon, reading the almanac, and then she died on Monday." Poor Mary, the thin volume was her sole library !

CHAPTER XVI. — It would involve a much more extended discussion than the space-limits of these notes will allow, to undertake to show the origin and meaning of the superstitions in regard to the sun and sunwise movement. While the origin and meaning of sun-worship has been very fully treated by Sir G. W. Cox, Professor Max Müller, Professor De Gubernatis, and others, the existence in modern times and among civilized communities of usages which seem to be derived from sun-worship has apparently almost escaped notice. I quote in this connection a few paragraphs from my brief article on this subject in the *Popular Science Monthly* for June, 1895 : —

" In dealing with the origination of actions or customs in which is involved what Dr. Fewkes calls the ceremonial circuit,[1] it is difficult to determine the value of the factor, whether it be large or small, that is due to the greater convenience of moving in a right-handed direction. Occasionally the dextral circuit is followed in cases in which it is evidently less convenient than the sinistral would be, as in dealing cards in all ordinary games. Also, who can tell just how large or small an element may depend upon the tradition that the left hand in itself is uncanny without reference to the sun's apparent motion ? There certainly is a general feeling of wide distribution that to be left-handed is unfortunate. Dr. Fewkes's careful and valuable researches among the Moki Indians of Arizona, however, show without doubt that they in their religious rites make the circuits sinistrally, *i. e.*, contrary to the apparent course of the sun, or, as physicists say, contra-clockwise. The Mokis also are careful to stir medicines according to the sinistral circuit. But doubtless instances go to show that among Asiatic and European peoples the general belief or feeling is that the dextral circuit — *i. e.*, clockwise, or with the apparent motion of the sun — is the correct and auspicious direction."

" As contra-sunwise notions were thought to be of ill omen or to be able to work in supernatural ways, so it came to be believed that to reverse other acts — as, for instance, reading the Bible or repeating the Lord's Prayer backward — might produce powerful counter-charms. The negroes in the Southern States often resort to both of these latter practices to lay disturbing ghosts. In the ring games of our school children they always move sunwise, though whether because of convenience or from some forgotten reason who can say ? "

[1] *Journal of American Folk-Lore*, vol. v. No. XVI. p. 33.

"In New Harbor, Newfoundland, it is customary, in getting off small boats, especially when gunning or sealing, to take pains to start from east to west, and, when the wind will permit, the same custom is observed in getting large schooners under way. So, too, in the Western Isles, off the coast of Scotland, boats at starting are, or at any rate used to be, rowed in a sunwise course to insure a lucky voyage."

"It will be noticed that in several of these cures, as well as in some of the charms already cited, no rule is given as to the direction to be followed in movement; but it is quite possible that the original description was more explicit, and it is almost certain that in every instance a sunwise course would now be followed."

No. 1166. — This appearance is due to the presence of a minute unicellular plant of a red color, which grows and multiplies with great rapidity on the surface of bread, starch-paste, and similar substances. So general was once the belief in its portentous nature that Ehrenberg described it under the name *Monas Prodigiosa.*

No. 1176. — The non-appearance of *rigor mortis* as omen of another death is alluded to in a skeptical way by Sir Thomas Browne in his *Vulgar Errors*, Book V. chapter xxiii.

No. 1280. — Doubtless this apparently most trivial and meaningless sign is but one of hundreds of examples of pure symbolism. The custom of draping the bell or front door-knob with crape when death has come to a house is suggested by seeing anything hung on the door-knob. It might be convenient to hang the dish-cloth to dry on the kitchen door-knob, as the door stands open. The idea of death is suggested, then comes the thought, "this is like death, hence it may bode death," and so the omen arises.

No. 1204. — See article on "Current Superstitions," *Journal of American Folk-Lore*, vol. ii. No. IV.

No. 1207. — Not infrequently people of education and culture feel that mourning is significant of further deaths. In popular arguments about the advisability of wearing mourning it is said that if one begins to wear it, he will have occasion to continue to do so. It is also claimed that mourning is directly unhealthful on account of injurious components of the black dyes used. This delusion no doubt proceeds from observed cases of ill-health due to the depressing effects of mourning upon the spirits (and therefore the physical condition) of the wearer.

No. 1237. — See "Current Superstitions," *Journal of American Folk-Lore*, vol. ii. No. IV.

I chanced to know a few years ago of a family party of educated, unusually intelligent people, when it happened that the number to dine was thirteen. One laughingly proposed to sit at a side table and did so. The dinner table would otherwise have been a bit crowded, the hostess said as excuse for heeding the evil omen of thirteen at table. I doubt if one of those present had any real faith in the superstition, and yet I fancy there was a certain feeling of relief in avoiding the augury predicted by the old saying.

No. 1241. — See article, "Survivals of Sun Worship," by the author, in *Popular Science Monthly*, June 9, 1895.

No. 1247. — To what extent an old custom of touching the dead survives I cannot say, but I well remember a painful experience of my own early childhood. I had been taken to the funeral of a little child, and at the proper time passed with the little procession to take leave of the dead baby. A lady who had charge of me turned down the wrist of my glove and bade me touch the corpse, which I did. At the time I felt it was to show me how cold were the dead, but I now think it must have been in conformity with some tradition, for the person who directed me was one who had great regard for what were deemed the proprieties in funeral rites.

Nos. 1335–1338. — It is quite a general custom among country people on the Eastern Shore of Maryland to decapitate a crowing hen. The same custom is reported from New Hampshire and from Prince Edward Island. Does not this proverb then refer to the common superstition that it presages death or disaster for a hen to crow, in consequence of which such hens are summarily killed?

No. 1415. — There is a somewhat widespread prejudice in the minds of old people against having their pictures taken, particularly if they have never done so. I do not think the objection is a natural conservatism, or dislike of doing something to which one is unaccustomed. The ill omen does not appear to have been feared for the young as well as for the old, even in provincial localities, when for the first time portraiture by daguerreotypy or more recently by photography was introduced. It has long been known that among primitive peoples there is a decided prejudice against portraiture. The notion seems to be that the individual may lose his vigor, if not his life, by allowing a copy of himself to be made in any way. Catlin in his intercourse with the North American Indians found great difficulty in gaining the consent of individuals to his painting them. He says in his work on *The Manners, Customs, and Condition of the North American Indians*, "The Squaws generally agreed that they had discovered life enough in them [Catlin's portraits] to render my medicine too great for the Mandans; saying that such an operation could not be performed without taking away from the original something of his existence which I put in the picture, and they could see it move, could see it stir." Herbert Spencer, in his *Principles of Sociology*, vol. i. p. 242, refers to a similar belief among the Chinooks and the Mapuchés. It would seem as if there is in the popular mind an instinctive recognition that the tenure of life is less strong in the aged than in the young. So while the general notion that it is dangerous to have one's person represented has disappeared from the mind of civilized man, a similar psychological condition survives here and there among people leading peculiarly simple lives.

Another evidence of a popular belief in some vital relationship between a portrait and its original is suggested by the quite general superstition that photographs (or other pictures) fade after and in consequence of the decease of the original. I have found this to be a common belief in

Ireland, Prince Edward Island, and in various parts of the United States. I remember as a child to have heard persons remark while turning over a family album of photographs, "That looks as if the person were dead." In fact, I think that I thus received the impression that the picture of one dead underwent some change that many persons could perceive and thus become aware of the death of the original. This notion is akin to a superstition of the Irish peasantry that the clothes left by the dead decay with unusual rapidity.

In parts of New Hampshire it is counted unlucky to have a photograph copied while the original lives. Is this because death is thereby suggested, since it is so customary to have enlarged copies of a photograph made after the decease of the original?